MANAGING CHANGE IN OLD AGE

SUNY Series in
Anthropology and Judaic Studies

WALTER P. ZENNER, EDITOR

MANAGING CHANGE IN OLD AGE

THE CONTROL OF MEANING IN AN INSTITUTIONAL SETTING

HAIM HAZAN

STATE UNIVERSITY OF NEW YORK PRESS

Production by Ruth Fisher
Marketing by Theresa A. Swierzowski

Published by
State University of New York Press, Albany

© 1992   State University of New York

For information, address the State University of New York Press,
State University Plaza, Albany, NY 12246

Library of Congress Cataloging-in-Publication Data

Hazan, Haim.
  Managing change in old age : the control of meaning in an
institutional setting / Haim Hazan.
      p.   cm. — (SUNY series in anthropology and Judaic studies)
  Includes bibliographical references and index.
  ISBN 0-7914-1063-3 (CH acid-free). — ISBN 0-7914-1064-1 (PB acid-free)
  1. Aged—Institutional care—Israel.   2. Aged—Israel—Attitudes.
3. Old age homes—Israel—Management.   I. Title.   II. Series.
HQ1064.I7H39   1992
305.26′09—dc20   91-26575
                                                                CIP

10 9 8 7 6 5 4 3 2 1

To the memory of my parents

David Hazan
1909–1978

Sima Hazan
1920–1989

Contents

LIST OF TABLES

Acknowledgments

Entering the realm of old age has been a lengthy and arduous journey. It began with extensive fieldwork commenced in the early seventies in an Israeli old-age home whose turbulent and unpredictable life was as surprising as it was indecipherable. The self-contradictory position of the residents as dependent and independent, active and passive, past-oriented and present bound, made the material intricate and intriguing, but also exceedingly problematic. The endeavor to introduce anthropological order into a seemingly unintelligible reality, aside from being an academic puzzle (see Postscript), is a personal feat. The elderly residents of the Home—a double-edged term for a self-subversive notion of "home"—were as confused as I with the presence of an unidentified stranger among them. The personnel were even more bewildered than the residents as to the purpose and the justification of the anthropological question. Suspicion, apprehension, and amusement were thus shared by all parties and the research ploded slowly along an obstacle race of misunderstandings and breaches in communication. Ultimately, trust and confidence were established in the course of intensive interactions and close encounters.

The process of confidence building was dovetailed by a tacit understanding that residents and staff alike were not to be implicated by publication of material of an apparent embarrassing nature. In respect of such wishes and in recognition of the plight of having to stage images of appropriate behavior for the prupose of survival at the Home, the material was belatedly published. All residents involved are out of the research arena and most members of the staff are presently out of duty. It, therefore, is a posthumous obligation to thank those who placed their trust in me and enabled the unfolding of life stories, social situations, and personal thoughts that lay the basis of the following ethnography.

Many colleagues were involved with the development of the manuscript. Professors S. Deshen, E. Marx, R. Shapira, and Mr.

Shokeid of Tel Aviv University made useful comments while Mrs. R. Bookstein and Mr. C. Keye helped with the initial preparation of the manuscript. I am particularly grateful to Mr. D. Glantz whose meticulous and insightful editing of the text brought it to its present form. Finishing touches and indexing were taken care of by Mr. A. Raz whose dedicated work is much appreciated. The Institute for Social Research and the Faculty of Social Sciences at Tel Aviv University provided funds for typing and other technical matters.

A very special tribute must be paid to Professor Victor Turner who, prior to his untimely death, took upon himself to read the first version of the manuscript and to contribute some of his immense knowledge and unique wisdom to its themes.

This book would not have been published without the trust and encouragement extended to me by my wife, Mercia, and without the patient endurance of our children Gil, Lee, and Dana.

PREFACE

Old men ought to be explorers
Here and there does not matter
We must be still and still moving
Into another intensity

T. S. Eliot*

Caught between fears and misconceptions, apprehensions and prejudice, the student of old age gropes his way in the unknown Country of the old. Equipped with a mental map, designed and sketched out by one generation of sociocultural gerontologists, someone searching for orientations and establishing bearings would find this to be a self-subversive enterprise, for the coordinates of such a map are charted on the basis of conflicting sets of assumptions.

The understanding of the aging process has been governed by two main perspectives. The first is hinged on the view that elderly people, having relinquished many of their social roles, and being treated by their social milieu in accordance with their seeming immediate needs, can be best understood in terms of the structure of their present lives. The second conception has advocated a diachronic approach whereby old peoples' lives are deemed to be strongly impinged upon by past experience and previous identities.

Notwithstanding the sociopsychological origins of these two referential scopes of aging, it is important to note that since they reflect a crucial contradiction in terms, it is academically incomprehensible, although scholastically plausible, to subscribe to both. Thus, gerontology has assumed a perennial cleavage between a diachronically underpinned life-cycle-based continuity and an environmentally conditioned, structurally determined present. With

---

*From "East Coker," in T. S. Eliot, *Four Quartets* (New York: Harcourt, Brace, 1943).

neither approach offering satisfactory explanations nor informing each other, any commitment to one of the two inevitably leads to a misguided view of aging.

The following is not intent on dismissing or demolishing either approach, nor is it an attempt to expound an alternative perspective. Rather, it is a reviewing of old age through the prism of the experience of change as an added existential dimension in both the construction and understanding of aging. Invested with the intricacies of this analytic focus, continuity, context-process, and structure will be fused to form a synchronically based framework of explanation.

The setting chosen as an arena for examining the arguments henceforth considered is an old-age home. It is the intense interplay of change-related factors in such social surroundings that directed attention to an anthropological inquiry into institutional life. Reconstructions of life histories, organizational processes, societal dynamics and, above all, the temporal dilemmas embedded in old age, render change in that environment salient, ubiquitous, and omnipotent.

The foci of the ethnography are the activities of three groups of residents in an Israeli old-age institution for the able-bodied. Through the application of participant observation methods, unstructured interviews with residents, members of the staff and visitors to the home, and written record analysis, a portrait of life in an institutional setting for the aged emerged. It became clear from the onset of the research that, contrary to common stereotypes, neither homogeneity of behavior nor uniformity of needs were to be found among the residents. However, when ethnographic accounts generated issues pertaining to the management of past experience and future plans vis-à-vis present conditions, a discernable pattern of managing change and time transpired. Notwithstanding the vast diversity of backgrounds and the heterogeneity of activity, the attitude towards change and the mode of action designed to handle it followed a regularized code of constituting reality.

It is that code and its constituents that this book is set to explore and elucidate. Challenging though it is for the understanding of human existence, the current study is confined to the account at hand. It remains to be seen whether the conclusions and implications withstand the scrutiny of comparable material and whether the open questions posed are taken up by further research. Only

xiv

within such a broader framework can the inquiry into the lives of the residents of such homes claim social universality or else remain a culturally unique enterprise in the experience of aging. Far from resolving this issue, the following endeavors to draw a modified mental map to guide the understanding of old age.

As we shall see, the locus of our interest is the arrest of change and the freezing of time. However, it is neither the transcendental sphere of temporality nor is it the biological cessation of existence that stand at the core of the ensuing account. Rather, it is the socially constructed, momentarily halted flow of change that prompts our attempt of looking at the lives of the aged through the prism of the dynamics of immutability. This is presumably the point to which Aldous Huxley suggests when he states:

> Thought is determined by life, and life is determined by passing time. But the dominion of time is not absolute, for "time must have a stop" in two senses, from the Christian point of view in which Shakespeare was writing. It must have a stop in the last judgement, and in the winding up of the universe. But on the way to this general consummation, it must have a stop in the individual mind, which must learn the regular cultivation of the mood of timelessness, of the sense of eternity.*

---

*"Shakespeare and Religion," in Julian Huxley, ed., *Aldous Huxley, 1894–1963* (London: Chatto and Windus, 1965).

INTRODUCTION — ON MANAGING CHANGE IN OLD AGE

Old-age homes are often conceived of as isolated social realities sequestrated from the outside world, displaying the well-recognized characteristics of total institutions. Brief encounters with such establishments usually confirm and deepen that impression. Such a concentration of physically and mentally impaired persons meeting the eye of the casual observer obscures the presence of nonobtrusive threads linking this reality of seeming despair and decline to the larger fabric of its extra-institutional social environment.

The home in question evinces two aspects of this type of linkage. First, there are interactional ties and exchanges between the residents and some of their prior institutional social environments, connections that are still often reinforced and intensified. Second, life in the institution can be viewed as an encapsulated panorama of the predicaments and paradoxes, dilemmas and decrements distilled in the state of being old, being a person, and being an old person (Keith 1982).

This dimension of institutional life constitutes the main theme underlying the main line of this book: my analysis views the home as being a well-defined, socially concentrated living situation providing an insight into some fundamental existential dilemmas in the life of all older people.

A cursory survey of the current psychosociological literature on old age unequivocally supports the observation that a major theme underpinning many of its research interests revolves around the relationship between the elderly and their physical/psychological/social milieu. It appears this preoccupation with "adaptation" or "adjustment" to later life has overridden almost any other questions on the subject.[1]

The very concept of accommodating oneself to certain environmental conditions, or being subjected to the coping requirements of a situation fraught with inexorable stresses and strains, is analytically anomalous. Treating any individual as an entity utterly distinct from their social surroundings is both theoretically invalid and empirically misleading. It is not only a distortion to project a social conception of the elderly as "a race apart" into a seemingly impartial discussion of the issue, but it also defeats any attempt to understand old age as an integral facet of the human experience. Based on unexamined assumptions, such perspectives implicitly and unwittingly support the widely accepted belief that the old are essentially different beings from the non-old. Furthermore, to view the process of aging only as an unending encounter between the individual and the impositions, afflictions, and constraints of old age, is merely to reduce the elderly to an imputed set of needs without recognizing and acknowledging their capacity and desire to create and sustain a meaningful existential world.[2]

An alternative perspective that takes into consideration these reservations should address itself to the process through which an elderly individual construes and constructs his existential conditions. It is, therefore, my contention that the understanding of such a process is to be sought in a heuristic, dialectical model consisting of two sets of factors, dynamically interwoven into the fabric of everyday behavior, by a single, central organizing principle.

Drawing on the commonly used analytic dichotomy between actions and meanings (or any of its multifarious conceptual variations[3]), the first set of factors consists of the reservoir of images, resources, and power structure in which a person is immersed and enmeshed. It is through this complex of factors that their actions and interactions are regulated, controlled, and accomplished. The second set includes those perceptual, cognitive, and emotional points of reference upon which one's symbolic code is constructed. For the sake of presentation, the following terms are coined to denote both sets respectively: the former is to be labelled "fields of control," whereas the latter will be referred to as "spheres of relevance." The interface between the two sets engenders the behavioral foundation for the emergence of analytic constructs such as "interactions," "situations," and "structures," which together map out the social construction of reality experienced by the individual.

How are those grossly oversimplified schematic generalizations pertinent to the case of the elderly? Rolelessness,[4] anomie,[5] deprivation of status,[6] and curtailment of power are just a few of the concepts employed by social gerontologists as analytic shorthand for the position of the aged in a complex society. Bracketing the theoretical adequacy and utility of these terms, it is clear they reflect a larger general phenomena, the paramount dimension of which is the occurrence of accelerated change and growing disorder in the lives of the elderly. Thus, both fields of control and spheres of relevance are embedded in such taken for granted gerontological concepts as dynamic elements of an indeterminant nature.

The juxtaposition of accelerating change and disorder in later life can be construed as a consequence of the incongruity between prevalent social definitions regarding old age as a static state, and the individual's everyday experience of often uncontrollable deterioration. In other transitions throughout the various perceived phases of the life span, personal experience is matched and reinforced by corresponding, socially prescribed symbolic codes and rules of conduct. Unlike this, however, the process of growing old is imbued with an increased incompatability between a social temporality that is conceived of as immobile and passive, and the dynamics of the individual's personal time.[7] Furthermore, in a society where change is favorably associated with youth, progress, and modernity, the ominous occurrence of undesirable, unwelcomed, negative transformations in old age poses a sharp and perplexing contradiction to a person's self-image and personal identity, based as it usually is on a sense of existential continuity in one's social world.

Thus, if aging is to be viewed, as some scholars suggest,[8] as a life's career, meaningfully interlinking past experiences with a present state, then the question of continuity and disengagement in one's identity becomes a vital and fundamental consideration for the understanding of the management of change among the aged.

Hence, the problems of coping with change constitutes the intermediary third element in the proposed model. I intend in the following chapters to explore the relations between spheres of relevance and fields of control, as regulated and molded by the existential experience of aged persons confronted with the problem of unarrested, imminent changes in their life situations. The social life in the institution under study contains a wide diversity of forms for handling change, and the objective of this research is to explore the strategies employed by the residents to accommodate their predicament of impending change in old age vis-à-vis their social resources, perceptions, and images.

Old-age homes have been the subject of research mainly as care environments providing medical and other facilities for the accommodation of elderly inhabitants. A great amount of this corpus of studies is socially reformist in orientation, and hence, highly critical of the abuse of human dignity[9] and the financial exploitation of the helpless.[10] Others investigate the scope and pervasiveness of the phenomena.[11] Very few researches, however, address themselves to the inner reality of such establishments, and those who do generally focus on either the symptoms of institutionalization, such as power and control,[12] or on the impact of such living arrangements on the behavior of residents.[13] Two exceptions should be noted: an ethnographic study of Jewish residents of an ethnic-centered Sephardic Home (Hendel-Sebestein 1979) and a detailed account of the daily life of inmates in a geriatric institution (Gubrium 1975). Notwithstanding the very significant differences between the two institutions, both studies concentrate on interactions and perceptions of reality among residents and staff. However, while the former stresses the importance of preexisting ties and associations to the creation of community life among the residents in spite of the institutional power structure, the latter examines processes and procedures of handling interactions and shaping situations within the context of everyday life in the establishment.

This study, while examining the interaction of extra-institutional contexts with sets of internal relationships, also focuses on a dimension that no earlier study seems to have taken into consideration: the meaning and the management of change among the residents of old-age homes. Although alluded to in some studies as an indication and predictor of impending death,[14] it has not been conferred the pivotal significance it undoubtedly deserves. With the exception of Marshall (1979), Myerhoff (1979), and Hazan (1980a), which are all studies of noninstitutionalized age-homogenous communities, the association between leaving a care establishment and the fear of death has not been explored. The home in question lends itself to a focused analysis of the phenomenon of change since it confronts its residents with a set of constraints that turns removal into an omnipotent and ubiquitous possibility. But, unlike other forms of impending uncertainty, the mode of change in the home was conceived of and rendered manipulable. Thus, it could be transformed from an empirically observable social reality into the thematic organizing principle of this ethnography.[15]

It is my conviction that the quest of such an organizing principle is of supreme importance in social gerontology, for it can liberate the field from being either preoccupied with aging as a social problem, or as a random conglomeration of facts and figures rationalized by sociological constructs. The anthropology of aging has made significant strides in this direction by putting ethnographic research on the elderly on a par with other issues of traditional interest to the discipline.[16] The ethnographer's close-up perspective is not only imperative for the elimination and eradication of prejudice and misconceptions, but also for uncovering the fundamental codes guiding human behavior. It is the ultimate objective of this book to contribute toward such an accomplishment.

In the beginning, the book deals with the environmental conditions that constitute the physical, organizational, and to a certain extent, the social boundaries of the home. This is followed by two chapters discussing respectively the residents' spheres of relevance and fields of control. The subsequent three chapters examine the activities within three different groups of residents. The underlying argument being pursued is that the manipulation of control and relevance is interlocked with the attempts to arrest change when it is encountered. When and where relevance is tantamount to control, and vice versa, a state of immobility is reached. This idea, pursued throughout the book, will receive its final theoretical consideration in the concluding chapter.

1. The Setting

The transition of an aged individual from a community-oriented lifestyle to an institutional setting is a process constrained by a complex set of environmental factors. The bureaucratic, organizational arena within which the Home operates—the physical surroundings, the material conditions and the services in the institution—all represent predetermined circumstances that the prospective resident must confront. This is not to suggest these factors are immutable or invariant; in point of fact, few of these facets of institutional life are beyond the resident's potential manipulative powers. The period of an applicant's candidacy and the ensuing formal institutionalization inculcate in the resident the import of such factors as key components in the composition of his existential world. But by means of ongoing reinterpretation and constant cognitive reorganization of these elements, the conception of preset environmental boundaries is vitiated, imparting the process of delineating them with a strong sense of dynamics.

It is, therefore, incorrect to assume that factors such as physical and bureaucratic boundaries, as well as different material conditions, diverse as they are vis-à-vis individual residents and specific situations, are inevitably barriers or contradictory to social interaction. The purpose of this chapter is to specify these determinants and to assess the relative impact each of them has on institutional life and on the construction of the residents' fields of influence and spheres of relevance.

The interactions occurring inside an old-age home are not solely connected to the social contacts created within it, but are also dependent upon additional factors that construct the reality confronting both staff and residents. Such factors as the national provision of bed space for the elderly, the organizational bodies dealing with sheltered housing, and the physical conditions of the specific old-age home itself bear on the induction of the individual and their later experiences within the institution. It is possible to classify these factors according to both their physical distance from the institution and the extent to which individuals can influence and direct them to their needs. It is clear, for instance, that residents cannot relieve the pressure for admission to old-age homes by new applicants (although a planned change in attitude on the part of the aged, their families, and public bodies could effect such a result). On the other hand, it is easier to suppose that certain changes in the structure and services of the old-age home could be influenced by the desires of residents and staff.

/

"It is clear . . . that in the coming years the problem of the aged in our country is likely to worsen quantitatively without however reaching really alarming proportions" (Bachi 1971, 14).

What was the nature of this "problem" at the time of the research cited? How did it express itself in numbers? Was there a correlation between the problem and applications to old-age homes? These questions will provide a basis for understanding the institution studied within the network of agencies dealing with old age in Israel.

The proportion of the aged in the population (men over sixty-five, women over sixty) is increasing rapidly: in 1968 it was 3.8%, in 1961—5.3%, 1970—7.2%, and in 1980—8.6% (Brookdale 1982).

In Tel Aviv, the city where the old-age home is located, the aging of the indigenous population exceeds the national average due to the out-migration of younger elements and to a lower rate of population growth. It has been reported to be 4.4% in 1948, 5.9% in 1961, 10.5% in 1972 and 19.4% in 1983 (Statistical Abstract of Israel, 1972, 1975, 1978). Forecasts indicate a continuation of this trend.

Can it be concluded from these statistics that there will be a growing demand for admission to old-age homes? In the opinion of the authorities in the home under study, this is indeed the reason why they are unable to respond to the many requests for admission referred to them. The manager of the body that finances the home claims a backlog of some two thousand applicants[1] (Kenan 1973, 18).

An opposing trend, however—namely, a declining demand for admission, despite increased life expectancy—may be suggested by another indicator. This is the tendency of various bodies[2] involved in

2

the affairs of the aged to maintain the would-be applicant for as long as possible in the community, and to admit him only if his well-being is under severe threat. A Ministry of Welfare-sponsored survey in 1972 stated:

> The aim of the Ministry is to create conditions which enable the elderly to function with maximum independence within the framework of his family and his community and to meet his needs only when he requires a protected or institutional framework.
>
> For this purpose supportive community services are being established today to cater for the social and personal needs of the elderly, such as: special medical and social services, hot meals, social and occupational activities in 100 clubs and community centres in which 12,000 elderly persons participate and some 800 enjoy a daily hot meal. (Israeli Government Yearbook 1972, 267)

The Interministerial Committee on matters concerning old age stated in its 1967 report: "Only where living independently . . . becomes impossible or undesirable should the old person be considered a candidate for a protected existence in an institution" (Zilberstein 1967, 127).

Supporting this position, the director-general of Malben asserts, "A 65-year-old does not need to run into the nearest old-age home," and that half the present Malben population could still benefit from a community framework. In his opinion, the healthy aged have no place in an old-age home (Stern 1972, 16).

At the same time, it is necessary to point out that there was a general lack of awareness about the need for developing community services for the aged in Israel until the beginning of the seventies. Only scant public resources were allocated for such purposes. This is explained both by the fact that the percentage of the aged in the population was then comparatively low, and also due to the limited impact of the aged on the Israeli political scene.

Since the bulk of the elderly arrived in Israel with the waves of mass immigration at the beginning of the fifties, their involvement in the loci of political power was rather marginal. To this must be added the Israeli national ethos that sanctifies youth—associated with bravery—an ethos that arises from special needs of the State,

3

expressing itself in national festivals, in the educational system, and in the communications media. Thus, the Israeli old person is often left isolated and rejected, not only from his family and sources of livelihood, but also from the culture around him. Entrance into an old-age home signs and seals this self-image. This may help explain the fear and repugnance of the identification entailed in residence in an institution for the aged.

For example, an official survey showed that most older people with comparatively high incomes and of western origin (who constitute the majority of the population in the institution under study) do not seek institutional care. Only five percent in this category showed positive interest (Nathan 1970, 138).

Why, then, was the waiting list for the home under study so long? There is a number of reasons. Foremost among them is the desire of the applicants' families to rid themselves of their bothersome elderly. Other reasons are to be found in the institutional structure of the care for the elderly in Israel. Several factors affect the readiness and ability of the elderly persons and their family to choose a particular old-age home; one is the nature of the home from the standpoint of the level of its services and the living expenses incurred in residence there. Another factor is the linkage of the institution to some public body, which limits in advance the old person's choice of old-age home.

Most of the old-age homes at the time of this study were publicly owned, and the provision of beds for the elderly was principally under the jurisdiction of these bodies. Such institutions define their category of suitable candidates according to the principles of the body which supports them. Thus, for example, "Malben" cares for new immigrants only, "Landsmanshafter" caters to applicants of particular ethnic origin, while the "Mishan" network accepts only Histadrut members or their parents. The government itself does not operate any old-age homes.

To this must be added the 590 beds in geriatric hospitals and in geriatric wards of general hospitals.

The institutions belonging to the public and municipal authorities do not demand a particularly high entry fee and are at the same time of a reasonable standard. The private institutions that do not set up formal barriers of membership for admission are divided into two types: those offering a high level of services in exchange for considerable sums, beyond the reach of most of the public, and those

Table 1 Old-Age Institutions and Number of Beds in 1972

AFFILIATION	NO. OF INSTITUTIONS	ABLE-BODIED	NO. OF BEDS INFIRM	NO. OF BEDS BED-RIDDEN	TOTAL
Malben	6	1017	752	365	2134
Mishan	5	1240	—	—	1240
Immigrant Associations	5	335	45	35	415
Municipalities	3	237	221	103	561
Other Public Institutions	24	1351	284	269	1904
Total	43	4180	1302	772	6254
Private	34	1085	1054	—	2139
Grand Total	77	5265	2356	772	8393

(Weihl et al. 1970)

accepting modest payment but "whose level of physical and care facilities are of an extremely low order" (Zilberstein 1967, 132), or in cruder journalistic jargon: "moldy doss-houses" (Tal 1973, 12). The importance of private old-age homes is growing with the increasingly severe shortage of beds provided by the public sector.

The report of the Interministerial Committee on matters concerning old age proposes the number of beds per room as an index of the quality of treatment of the aged in Israel. According to this yardstick, thirty percent of the total number of beds are in four-bed rooms and twenty percent in three-bed rooms. "It appears then that about half the beds satisfy neither acceptable standards in developed countries nor the demands of the aged in Israel, the decisive majority of whom want a room to themselves"[3] (Zilberstein 1967, 129).

Another consideration with which the old person has to contend is the readiness and capacity of the institution to take care of him during illness or deterioration in his physical state. Three categories are commonly used to delineate according to the physical

5

state of the elderly person: "bedridden"—requiring constant medical attention and supervision; "infirm"—requiring regular medical assistance and functioning only with the help of auxiliary aids; and "able-bodied"—capable of functioning without help (Zilberstein 1967, 46–47). (Some institutions do not accept applicants in the "bedridden" or "infirm" categories or who are likely to become so shortly.) Accordingly, three types of institutions exist: those catering to all three categories, those admitting only the infirm or bedridden—usually geriatric wards in hospitals—and those designated only for the able-bodied.

The institution researched here is of the last type. An elderly person who is not able-bodied cannot be considered a candidate for admission, and an existing resident whose physical state has deteriorated can be transferred according to a contract signed in advance between the management and the individual's family.

Most of the facilities available for the bedridden are to be found in the institutions of Malben, which were originally intended for new immigrants only. Consequently, the facilities available for the indigenous aged population are very limited. It was this group that made up the candidature for the home studied. Here, the shortfall in beds was estimated to be 2550–2650 in 1972 (Librach 1974, 50). Acknowledgement of this statistic is essential to understanding the problem of "functioning," which will be discussed in a later chapter.

Mishan—the body to which the institution belongs—is, in fact, the only example of its type embodying this approach. As such, this policy has been the subject of debate between Mishan's leading representatives and functionaries of other institutions. It is worthwhile outlining some aspects of the debate, not the least because the matter of transfer from the institution is crucial to an understanding of what follows. In the terminology of the home's director, a framework accepting only one type of applicant can be called "homogeneous." In his opinion, the situation to be aspired to is of "a homogenous institution within a heterogeneous framework." That is, a system enabling the transfer of the resident to a more suitable institution when their unsuitability for the existing framework is determined.

Before discussing how this situation expresses itself in reality, we shall try to describe in general terms the process Mishan went through to arrive at its present-day arrangement. For this purpose we will be aided by the summary of Mishan activities as outlined in the report of the Interministerial Committee on matters concerning

6

old age. Mishan is a mutual aid society of the Histadrut (National Federation of Labor Unions), created to care for, among others, aged members of the Histadrut and their parents. Towards this end, it has been involved in several housing schemes for the aged:

Mishan began its operations in the housing sphere in 1958. The process of establishing suitable housing for the aged went through three stages. Firstly, Mishan acquired 70 apartments in high-rise buildings scattered throughout the Katamon district of Jerusalem. Each flat consisted of one large room, a hall, a kitchen with eating area, toilet facilities, and verandas. In one of the apartment buildings a social center, club, clinic, office and the manager's living quarters were located. All the flats were occupied by retired Histadrut members.

With the aging and accompanying physical decline of these individuals, the distance between their flats, dispersed throughout the neighborhood, made it difficult for them to reach the social center, as walking there to participate in cultural activities or to visit the clinic became progressively more onerous. As a result of this experience, Mishan embarked on a second stage which involved the establishment in Ramat Gan (near Tel Aviv) of a concentration of three-story buildings, each containing 150 flats. The tenants had at their disposal extensive, centralized facilities. Here mutual aid amongst the residents developed, finding its expression in a variety of ways. The large number of residents facilitated the development of wide-ranging activities, of both cultural and occupational nature, through the formation of different interest groups. Thus, the tenants were able to live independently, albeit under supervision. However, with the lessening of the elderly individuals' capacity to function, it became necessary to transfer them to an old-age home. This situation prompted the third stage of Mishan's program—housing in the vicinity of an old-age home, with the aim of allowing tenants to use the full range of centralized services to be found in an old-age home. Mishan is building in Holon an apartment house next to an old-age home with 150 beds. Efal comprises 6 residential blocks with many hundreds of beds and is situated next to an old-age home. Contrariwise, Mishan is building a new 200-bed old-age home

7

in Katamon, Jerusalem, to "cover" the aforementioned flat development dispersed throughout the neighborhood. Finally it is developing a 350-bed old-age home in Ramat-Aviv." (Zilberstein 1967, 117–118)

To this should be added that at the time of the study Mishan was building a 380-bed home for the chronically infirm to provide a framework that would absorb those no longer acceptable to "able-bodied" institutions (Kenan 1973, 19). The old-age homes presently run by Mishan are of three types (all containing able-bodied only): "individual" homes where the residents look after themselves in separate housing units; "collective" homes, in which most of the residents' needs are met by the institution; and "mixed" homes comprising a "collective" home, sited next to an "individual" home, which can utilize the services of the former.

As mentioned earlier, an argument persists as to which path to follow in the planning of institutions for the aged. The Welfare Ministry states that "special attention will be paid to ensuring a level of services for the elderly who are residents of institutions for the able-bodied in order to make it necessary to transfer them to institutions for the chronically sick as a result of deterioration in their health" (Israeli Government Yearbook 1972, 267). The Interministerial Committee on matters concerning old age, reporting on the Mishan approach, feels that "the most obvious flaw in its design is the lack of thought given to the old person when he becomes infirm or bedridden and has to be uprooted and transferred to one of the private hospitals for the chronically sick" (Zilberstein 1967, 118).[4] The report then adds: "Most geriatricians today believe that everything should be done to enable old people to lead an independent life in the community and as far as possible to participate actively in communal life" (Zilberstein 1967, 118). The conclusion to be drawn from the synthesis of both of these standpoints is, in the words of the report: "Formerly able-bodied residents now more infirm should be assured of their continued residence within able-bodied homes" (Zilberstein 1967, 134). Another voice supporting this view is the head of the Mental Health Services of the Health Ministry, because of the "anxiety and fears . . . as a result of the 'removal' of the old person in the case of illness" (Arkin 1973, 33).[5]

How has Mishan reacted to these changing ideas? The construction of an institution for the chronically ill is one response to

8

the problem, giving credence to the ideal of "a homogeneous institution within a heterogeneous framework." Mishan's management have presented yet further arguments: for example, the director of Mishan said in a newspaper interview:

> In a symposium held recently on the planning and management of old-age institutions, experts expounded the general conclusion that there is a need to separate the sick aged from the able-bodied. The experts emphasized that care should be taken that the healthy old person is not confronted on a daily basis by what is likely to happen to him. (Kenan 1973, 18)

In another context the same individual asserted:

> The care of the sick aged is the exclusive domain of medical institutions and of "Kupat Holim" (the Sick Fund), and Mishan cannot keep such patients under its auspices, due to the lack of suitable conditions for systematic medical care and a qualified team for treating the sick and incurable. These patients need for their own sake and for that of those around them a special framework, temporary or permanent. The atmosphere in an old-age home is invigorating, joyful and full of life. The elderly are busy with handicrafts, developing different hobbies, organizing social activities and spending time reading, writing, studying, playing, listening to the radio, watching films, having parties and going on trips. This framework is appropriate only for the able-bodied, who are able to look after themselves or require only minimal help and who are still able to enrich their lives substantively. In contrast, the elderly sick are not capable of doing this and not only do they remove themselves naturally from the normal routines of the institution, but they are also liable to lower the morale of the able-bodied around them making their lives more difficult by reminding them by their very daily presence of what could, perhaps, also befall the healthy. (Weiner 1968, 34)

A comparison of the arguments put forward by the proponents of this view with those of its dissenters reveals that both parties use the assumed mental state of the aged residents as the sole justification for their claims. Reality is far more complex, and financial,

9

administrative and organizational problems undoubtedly underlie both sets of attitudes.

With this background, it is possible to summarize the various factors creating pressure on the institution being investigated:

1) A very large number of potential applicants—Histadrut members and their parents.
2) Its location in the central region of Israel, where the percentage of the aged in the population is higher than elsewhere in the country.
3) The comparatively low maintenance payment demanded by the home, which is within the means of most of the aged, even without additional family assistance.[6]
4) The attraction that the home offers only one or two-bed rooms.
5) Because of the composition of its resident population and its attractive physical appearance, the home is considered to be quite a prestigious institution (by the Mishan directorate itself, as well).
6) Its position in the heart of a residential area allows easy access to various services and to nearby residential areas.
7) Other options available to older persons are, as we have seen, very limited due to the conditions of admission to other homes and because of the type of care offered by some of them.

As the result of this pressure, a situation is created having profound implications for what occurs within the institution, and in terms of our particular interest, the social organization of life within the home. The resulting imbalance between supply and demand constitutes a dynamic element not necessarily operating in the residents' favor. Thus, in any given case, it is liable to alter their current life situation in the home, which is perceived by them as a lesser evil than the alternative of being transferred to another institution.

II

The aim of this discussion is to highlight one of the main difficulties faced by the residents, the analysis of which will provide a fuller

10

picture of behavior in an old-age home. In the previous section, it was stressed that the home accepts only the able-bodied elderly and that residents whose physical or mental state has deteriorated are transferred. What then are the formal and informal requirements and rules for admission to and removal from the institution? How do these procedures influence the composition of the institution's population? These two key questions will be discussed in this section.[7]

The affiliation of the home to the Mishan system defines the first condition for the admittance of any new resident. The candidate must be a Histadrut member, or the parent of a member. All applications for admission are submitted for consideration to the Admissions Committee, chaired by the general director of Mishan, and of which the director of the home also serves as a member. A candidate accepted by the committee must still receive a final, formal approval by the home's director. The explicit criteria informing the decision are based on the level of the candidate's "functioning." As will soon be clarified, the definition and precise nature of this ability will be decisive in shaping the processes of social negotiation within the institution.

The elements informing this concept are of two sorts: those stated by the management and those not elaborated and not appearing in the institutional regulations, but whose importance is no less than that of the former. As was seen in the previous section, this old-age home accepts only the able-bodied, who are sufficiently ambulatory so as not to be "a bother" to the public. Another factor in the definition of a candidate's functioning is his or her ability to enter into the social life of the institution and to sustain normal personal relations with their neighbors. As indicated, the director is the final arbiter of the acceptability of a candidate. His decision is based on the report of the home's physician, and on a short interview conducted with the old person covering formal points pertaining to the presumed desire of the candidate to become integrated into the social life of the home. The director operates on the explicit assumption that, in his words: "There are people who are pearls in the home's crown"; namely, residents whose very presence enhances the place, regardless of their formal "functioning."[8] Another central, although implicit factor influencing the acceptability of an applicant is the individual's ability to expedite their admission by exploiting contacts outside the home, principally in the Histadrut, to exert the necessary pressure. This state of affairs is common knowledge to the

11

residents, and those who have gained admission thus do not even bother to hide it. On the contrary, they are generally proud of the fact. An understanding of this pride is complex and is implicit, together with several other factors, in the criteria employed by the residents for their mutual evaluations of each other. Nevertheless, the main factor is their relations with the management and the fear of possible "expulsion." This fear is enhanced by their awareness of the great pressure exerted to gain admission, as a result of the increasing demand for places in the home. (For every available bed, there are usually four candidates, who are suitable from a "functioning" standpoint.) Consequently, it should be clear that in order for the director to resist this pressure, which continually arises from the contacts made by new candidates with key officials of the Histadrut, he is obliged to remove as large a number as possible of "nonfunctioning" aged as often as possible.

Those residents who gained admission by exploiting their outside contacts are not fearful of a deterioration in their functioning, for their definition differs from the official definition. Others, however—mainly the initial intake of the home, when existing pressures had not yet crystallized—are constantly made conscious of the possibility of their removal and are apprehensive about being declared "dysfunctional" by the director. The director actually confirmed this when he stated: "When I see someone who is not moving well or who doesn't show up in the dining room for a long time, I keep an eye on him." Many residents go out of their way to demonstrate proper functioning, and one forum is by way of group activity. These variations in the definition of "functioning" (to be detailed later on) constitute the central variable in the determination of social relations within the institution.

In the contract signed between the management of Mishan and the resident and their family, the responsibility for hospitalization of the aged person rests with the family, with the home only promising help to facilitate arrangements for a later admission to a suitable institution. The maintenance costs in such institutions are usually considerably higher than that in the home being studied, and therefore this gives rise to resistance on the part of the family— which is in turn passed on to the resident themself—against transfer to another institution. In addition to this, there is the difficulty and bother of organizing the transfer—the aged person's induction into yet another new framework—and their severance from the so-

12

cial life of the present institution. Finally, there is the awareness that an (undisclosed) future in another institution denotes physical deterioration, a reduction of self-esteem, and increased uncertainty. From this brief initial sketch, it is clear that the concept of "functioning" varies from resident to resident[9] and that the criteria for accepting candidates on the one hand, and for removing them on the other, influence the makeup of the home's population. The composition of the home's population itself can be gleaned from the data presented in tables 4 and 5. In order to emphasize the specific character of the institution from the standpoint of its inhabitants, they are presented together with data on the noninstitutionalized elderly and also with those in other institutions[10] (the data are in percentages dating from 1971).[11]

The pronounced differences in the proportion of men to women outside institutions compared to that which obtains inside are the result of many of the basic reasons for entering an old-age Home. These reasons, as far as Israel is concerned, often derive from feelings of loneliness and powerlessness resulting from the death of a spouse (Nathan 1970, 138). Since the life expectancy of women in Israel is greater than that of men (Israel Statistical Annual 1970, 91), the proportion of women residents in institutions is also higher.

The percentage of residents in the home, whose age is between sixty and sixty-nine, is double that of other old-age homes, and represents almost half of those existing in the noninstitutionalized aged population. This indicates that old people in this age range who do not require hospitalization and special care are to be found in this home more than in other institutions. But at the same time, their

Table 2   Distribution of Aged According to Place of Residence and Sex

PLACE OF RESIDENCE	SEX		TOTAL
	M	F	
Institution studied	33.3	66.7	100
Other institutions	33.3	66.7	100
Not in institutions	49	51	100

Table 3   Distribution of Aged According to Place of Residence
and Age (In Percentages)

RESIDENCE	AGE					TOTAL
	60–69	70–79	80–89	80+	90+	
Institution studied	20	62	16.7		1.3	100
Other institutions	10	44		45		100
Not in institutions	44	45		11		100

proportion in the institutionalized population is no less than that of
the noninstitutionalized aged population. The "functioning" syndrome helps to explain this unusual phenomenon. Ordinarily, this
age group does not tend to enter institutions because most of its
members are still tied to their families, and in many cases, even to
their jobs. In comparison, an absolute majority of the home's residents come from the seventy to seventy-nine age range. These are
the "able-bodied" elderly whose ties with their families are weaken-
ing and for whom managing household chores has become a strain.
This cohort is not in the majority in other Homes where the eighty
plus age group is larger. The reason for this is clear: the eighty plus
group are more prone to deterioration in their physical condition
(Zilberstein 1967, 50), and therefore, they have at the same time less
chance of admission to a home and a greater propensity to be removed from it. The low percentage of old-age home residents in this

Table 4   Distribution of Aged in the Home Studied—According
to Year of Immigration

	YEAR OF IMMIGRATION		TOTAL
	Before 1948 (Including Native-Born)	After 1948	
In the home studied	72.2	27.8	100

(Available comparative data insufficient)

14

Table 5 Distribution of Aged in the Institution and Outside It According to Country of Origin (In Percentages)

PLACE OF RESIDENCE	COUNTRY OF ORIGIN					
	Israel	Europe	America	Balkan[13]	Asia-Africa	Total
The home	3.5	71	0.8	17.7	7	100
Other institutions	4	70			26	100
The non-institutionalized	4	67			29	100

age group is explained by a relatively high death rate (Bachi 1971, 15) and by the fact that a large number are hospitalized.

The high percentage of "veterans" (early Zionist immigrants, usually of European background) is also explained by the nature of this particular home, affiliated as it is to the Histadrut and considered by its leading lights as a prestigious institution, to which admission can be obtained with the help of the relevant officials with senior standing in the parent organization.[12] It is also possible that the maintenance payment required, although not considered unduly large, effectively bars that section of the non-"veteran" population who are unable to afford such payments (Weihl et al. 1970, 218). Another reason for the small number of post-1948 immigrants among the residents is the existence of Malben—an organization designated exclusively for the immigrant aged. Support for the contention that the home does not contain a specific type of population—Jews from the Oriental communities, and especially those who arrived after 1948—can be found in table 7.

A significant difference exists mainly between the proportion of those of Afro-Asian origin in the general aged population and their proportion in the home. The seven percent that are nevertheless present are almost always "veterans" in the country with a history of participation in public affairs or, alternatively, they are the parents of individuals with connections and status. Characteristic also is the small number of American-born residents. This group, despite being relatively well-off, does not enjoy close personal ties with Histadrut personalities, while at the same time those with

15

independent means can apply to old-age homes demanding higher fees.

The special composition of the home's population can also be understood in terms of the nature of the Oriental family structure, which facilitates care of the elderly at home. It thus postpones institutional care until a later stage and, in many cases, never seeks it at all. Nevertheless, it seems that the social network of the family—that is, the extent of connections in the Histadrut—overrides the importance of family structure or life-style in reaching the decision and enabling the possibility of placement of the aged family member in an institution.

Another essential datum for the understanding of the home is not included in this chapter because the management has no interest in its dissemination. These are the figures relating to turnover in the home—the numbers transferred, the numbers entering the institution by "queue jumping," and the chronological correlation between these sets of data. All that can be said is that the number of residents leaving the home—up to and including the period of study—of their own free will and not as a result of a deterioration in functioning—was twenty, while the number of those who died after being transferred was twenty-four. Deaths within the home were rare and were generally the result of accidents or suicide, since dying residents were transferred from the home before the actual onset of death.

The reluctance to provide information on those dying is not exclusive to the management. Residents also avoid the subject, albeit for different reasons. The mere mention of death and its incipience may impair the defense mechanisms described below. Management and residents alike adopt avoidance behavior with respect to this pivotal fact of institutional life, but for wholly different motives and interests. Parallel patterns of behavior of this type characterize many dimensions of institutional interaction and will be revealed as foci in the negotiating processes described later.

III

When new residents are admitted to the home they encounter a number of factors that affect their life there. At this stage of the analysis, we are not concerned with the people they meet and with whom they will develop reciprocal relations, but rather with the material conditions that determine how their daily needs will be met. In this section, the physical structure of the building and its effect on the lives of the residents will be described, together with the standard services provided by the home and the daily routine by which they are dispensed.[14]

The old-age home is concentrated in a single high-rise building located in a highly populated residential area in one of Tel Aviv's most prestigious neighborhoods. A short distance from the gate a supermarket is to be found, where the elderly can buy food and thus lessen to some extent their dependence on the home's offerings, as well as extending their freedom of choice regarding both the nature of their food and the times at which it is served.

Several bus-stops on the road that surrounds the building facilitate regular access to all parts of the city and even further afield. This is an important point in relation to one of the main criteria defining a total institution: ". . . all aspects of life are conducted *in the same place* and under the same single authority" (Goffman 1961a,b; my emphasis).

The residents who are "able-bodied," that is, enjoying total mobility, can visit their families and friends, sleep outside the home on occasion, shop, and take part in social and recreational activities being held in town. Not everyone takes advantage of these opportunities to the same extent and, as will become clear shortly, this is one of the major yardsticks for distinguishing between various groups and individuals within the home.

The building is surrounded by lawns that are widely utilized. Dotted along the paths are a few worn benches, exposed to the weather and therefore not heavily used. During evening hours, the residents and their visitors generally do not venture outdoors a great deal, which suggests the residents' preference for seclusion in the privacy of their own room rather than public exposure. Most of those making use of the benches are the residents of double rooms, some of whom have come to an agreement with their roommates regarding allocation of time to be spent alone in the room. Others find themselves abandoning their rooms at certain periods in response to pressure or disturbance inflicted upon them by their roommates.

The building itself is a stressed concrete structure with a smooth and polished exterior, recalling a modern hotel or office

17

building, with the concomitant impression of cleanliness and uniformity. Generally speaking, the building has been planned so that group activities are concentrated on the lower floors. The living quarters of the residents are located higher up, with those of the staff found on the uppermost floor.

The home has 260 rooms, of which 120 are single and the remainder double. The rooms are medium-sized, each with access to a corridor and a small veranda. The standard furnishings that are supplied by the home include, in addition to a bed, a table, two chairs, a cupboard, and a side table. Each room has toilet facilities, an internal phone, and central heating. Additional articles can only be brought into the room with the management's permission. Almost all the residents keep personal items in their rooms, some of them without permission. Radios are evident and television sets, installed by special permission only, are present to a lesser extent. Electrical cooking appliances are prohibited and a resident who wants a hot drink is obliged to utilize a thermos. This regulation results in the common sight of old people en route between their rooms and the first floor bearing thermos flasks that are often cracked and leaking. This phenomenon interferes with the institution routine to such an extent as to invite intervention from the management.[15] Candles cannot be lit in the rooms for fear of fire and this ruling, too, affects the residents' way of life, particularly the women, who are thus prevented from blessing the Sabbath candles in their rooms, and can only observe this ancient religious tradition in a specially designated area next to the manager's office. This attests to the extent to which a building's structure (where hundreds of people are concentrated), the physical state of its inhabitants (old people may stumble or tremble and drop the candle), and the nature of the institution (one with orders and regulations universally applicable to all) can influence the performance of symbolic behavior.[16]

The narrow corridors are suitable only for passage from the rooms to the showers and elevators. There is not enough space in the halls for residents to congregate, so social activity must necessarily take place either in bedrooms that are too small to hold more than a few people, or in specially designated areas on the lower floors. Each corridor has two wider areas around the elevator entrances and an internal phone for staff use. On every floor there are four showers, a single bath, and toilets. Incorporated in each corridor is a central waste disposal serving the rooms. Taking care of those disposal units is a vexing problem for management and residents alike.

18

The pressure on these various services is not equal, being concentrated during morning and evening hours as well as on Fridays. The time allocated to each user is not uniform. Some residents—because of their difficulty in functioning—need more time to care for their personal hygiene. Others see the use of services as a means of demonstrating independence, providing a framework for competition with other residents, as well as a "struggle" with the staff.

Stairs and security rooms are also found on each floor. Access between floors is facilitated by twelve elevators spread throughout the home. Due to the multistory nature of the building and the restricted mobility of many of its residents, use of the elevators is essential to the home's way of life. Two implications flow from the use of elevators by the residents and their dependence on them. Crowding into them, mainly before and after meals, makes for friction that sometimes graduates to quarrels or even to an exchange of blows. Entry and exit is often a slow business, and sometimes gives rise to tension and impatience, which lead to an exchange of unpleasant words. At the same time, since finding one's way around the building depends on how to use the elevators, and a resident cannot conduct an orderly routine without such familiarity, elevator rides have become a yardstick by which to evaluate the ability of the resident to acclimatize to the home. Thus, for example, a resident who is not able to find his way to the dining room is considered out of place in the home. This dependence on the elevators sharpens and exposes failings that in other circumstances might be minimized.

The two ground floors include the areas designated for group activities and the home's offices. The basement floor incorporates work rooms, a synagogue, a television and lecture room, a large concert hall, laundry, and a parking lot for the staff and residents.[17] This floor, with the exception of the work rooms, is utilized only in the afternoons and evenings. Here also, as is the case in the living quarters, group activity that is not planned in advance cannot be conducted, since the various areas mentioned have predefined functions for given needs and for specific residents.

The floor above—the main reception floor—includes several central features of the home, and therefore we will survey it in detail. One entrance leads to a lobby containing some tables and a large number of chairs and sofas. Here visitors can be received, one can wait before meals (although at this time the hall is so crowded that most of those waiting have to stand), gather in groups, or simply watch people coming and going. Some of the old people here do

19

not even bother to look around, instead gazing off into space or directing their attention to the floor without attempting to make contact with their surroundings (this subject will be discussed more fully in due course). This large area, which is undivided and unrecessed, invites self-exposure. In addition, there is the continual traffic of staff, alert to what is happening, and able to record the residents' behavior. Their impressions are important in determining how the resident is functioning. Thus the hall provides a stage for the demonstration of proper functioning, or conversely, for catching the resident "off guard" when misbehaving—below par in his or her functioning.

From the lobby one may go in any of three directions: to the dining room, to the management's offices, or to the clubroom. The dining room is locked between meals and getting into the kitchen requires a good deal of persuasion on the part of a resident. The tables seat eight and some of them are designated for those on special diets—vegetarians, diabetics, hypertensives, and so on. The diners all have their own seats, which cannot be changed without permission of the management. This is done to expedite supervision of absenteeism from the home: an empty place is thus immediately identified with a given resident. Mealtime is also when the manager makes his announcements to the residents. The dining room is a focus of attraction and interest for many residents—as well as for arousing a not inconsiderable amount of tension. It is not unusual for the table manners of one individual to be criticized by his neighbor, or the taste and quality of the food to become the subject of heated argument. Analysis reveals the evaluation of the food is closely linked to the resident's assessment of the management, and that compliments paid to the chef complement the praise extended to the manager and vice versa: criticism of dining-room procedures goes hand in hand with arguments against the management.[18] Another common phenomenon in the dining room is the transfer of food from the tables into a pocket, or previously prepared bag, to be taken to the resident's room where the contents are either eaten or may become moldy and be thrown away. It is possible that an explanation of this behavior may be found in the field of the psychology of old age (see, for example, Guttman 1969). But it seems more tenable to see it as a part of the residents' behavior pattern in a total institution with a compulsory framework, where in response to a sense of the negation of personal identity, the residents demonstrate their rebellion by means of acts of nonconforming behavior.

20

In reviewing the physical features of the building, a number of characteristics stand out—for example, the impossibility of organized activity except in the special areas designated by the management. The concentration of these activities on the two lower floors facilitates supervision of the residents by the staff, in terms of observation and even of intervention. Encounters between individuals are frequent, and despite the fact that not everyone knows one another, information about the presence of the others exists and has implications for the way the residents perceive the Home and their place within it. This especially applies to the group that sits in the lobby, in a state of inactivity for most of the day. These individuals, despite their inactivity, serve as a point of reference for the other residents. Another result of the architecture is its influence on the nature of communication between residents. The need for uniformity in the provision of services, for group activities, and the very fact of entering and leaving the building create frequent contacts between residents, and these encounters lead, in many instances, to conversations about different topics, mainly relating to the home itself. Such conversations are peppered with gossip about other residents and much of the information gleaned about others in the home is acquired in this fashion.

In the description of the building's structure mention was made of the services supplied by the home. Within this framework we will refer only to those services universally provided and not those specific to different groups. These basic services are food provision, cleaning facilities (living quarters, laundry), and the clinic. All other services depend on the desire and the ability of the recipient and the provider—thus watching a film, or taking part in a group are not directly imposed on anyone and physical well-being is not contingent on them. This means that the possibility of waiving participation in these activities or finding alternatives is greater than in the case of basic services.

The routine time schedules in the home are of two sorts: those where the residents must comply in order to avail themselves of the basic services, and those where this is not necessary. Meal times are fixed (at 8:30 A.M., 12:30 P.M., and 6:00 P.M.). The cleaning of rooms, performed systematically under the aegis of a responsible member of the staff, is also independent of the wishes of the residents, although it is possible for the work to be undertaken earlier by proffering gifts to the cleaning staff. The doctor also works regular hours. During the morning there are almost no organized activities except

21

for handicrafts. Most organized activities are carried out in the afternoon framework of interest groups. (As will be clarified later, participation in an interest group bestows certain advantages on the resident in the home.) This is also the usual time for family visits, and many old people are absorbed in conversation and in playing with their children and grandchildren. Old people in any old-age home find themselves in an institution that dictates a considerable part of their daily schedule and offers incentives for the way they spend the rest of their day. This organization of time is external or "objective" (Fontana 1976) and bears no clear connection to the subjective time-world of the residents themselves.

In fact, the emphasis on repetition and regularity in the daily routine is essential for an understanding of the reactions to change to be found among the residents. In addition to facilitating psychological security by offering "time-anchors" (Roth 1963) in a situation of uncertainty, this fixed schedule may be seen as an important resource for structuring a world that does not allow for deterioration or for unexpected and threatening changes.[19]

The organizational and physical boundaries of the home are not the same for all residents. We have seen that certain residents can circumvent the formal definition of functioning and yet still avoid living under the threat of possible removal (this topic will be developed in the next chapter), by means of their deftness in exploiting their connections with the bureaucratic organization within which the home operates. The material conditions existing in the home can be modified partly or wholly, so that the boundaries of daily life for the residents are not standardized for everyone, but are dependent on the mobility of the old person, their family's support, and their economic standing. These variables provide only a partial explanation for the different grades of relative totality; the main factors, to be elucidated in the following chapters, will concentrate on the social relations constructed within the home, relations that to a large extent determine the nature and level of totality to which any given resident is subject.

22

2. SPHERES OF RELEVANCE

The physical and organizational boundaries of the old-age home constitute one set of factors, but not necessarily the pivotal axis in shaping the residents' social construction of reality. Admission to the institution and residence there stamps the inhabitants with the social stigma of being the unwanted aged. Such labelling has wide-ranging implications for their self-perception and for the network of social relations in which they are enmeshed. The very fact that the home is open, access to it convenient, and there is an absence of any genuine physical limitations or barriers to maintaining contact with the outside world, creates a set of dilemmas for the residents, which might not be felt so acutely in a closed or more isolated institution.

This potential freedom of choice the residents ostensibly enjoy provides for flexibility in their determination of personal time priorities and spheres of content, according to noninstitutional criteria. In other words, the fact that the resident is not totally and constantly exposed to her institutional environment may nurture in her the belief that she can continue to adhere to those patterns of meaning that informed and represented the center of gravity of her life-world, before entering the home. This creates a focus of conflict between her previous identity and the reality of the home, demanding confrontation with situations and social relations that do not necessarily derive from or suit her earlier spheres of relevance. This is not just an ordinary situation, of transition from one structured social reality to another, but of entry into a new existential reality that lacks an identity structure. The social situation of the resident before entering an old-age home is often characterized by a damaged self-image and sense of alienation, accompanying the loss of prior ties and identities. An old-age home itself is not a framework whose explicit or implicit purpose is the fashioning of a new identity, so that the resident finds themself trapped in a world of nonexistent or contradictory categories. This creates for them a world whose major characteristics are paradox and lack consistency. It is not a world deficient in content or standards, for on the contrary, it boasts a multiplicity of references and interpretations, but they do not make for a limited and crystallized understanding of an existential order. Moreover, while in the day-to-day world outside the home the various and varied levels of ordinary daily experience, which are not necessarily compatible with each other, are differentiated by defined areas of time, action, and place, such boundaries do not exist within the home. Thus, a reality is created where boundaries are blurred, both between different levels of reference and also within them.

Clearly, no uniformity exists within the "substantive" lifeworlds of the residents, and the dilemma that faces them as residents in the home is, in large measure, the result of differences between them. At the same time, there are a number of areas in which it is possible to locate common foci both for similarities and for divergence. These areas do not incorporate all the existential alternatives that emerge in the institution, but these assume a decisive importance in the structuring of all of the residents' social reality.

The analysis of the categories that make up the resident's world will be developed through an investigation of the systems of social relations in which they are found. The assumption underpinning this approach is that cultural categories have no independent existence except insofar as they constitute part of the social reality that they shape and by which they in turn are shaped. In other words, a dialectic process interweaves worlds of meaning explicated in the course of interaction between concrete situations and social relations on the one hand, with theoretical conceptions—and the relevant scholarly literature—on the other.

The sociological and anthropological literature dealing with the phenomenology of old age is quite sparse[1] and presently inadequate to help delineate the boundaries of the likely categories making up the world of old people, especially since the assumption of universalism of this world for all of the aged is exaggerated and does not bear the scrutiny of existing comparative research. Consequently, the source of the following empirical generalizations emerges from the field itself. At the same time, it is facile to ignore the existence of a common denominator between the system of categories observed in the institution and the problems and patterns of generalized reference perceived as characterizing old age and old

24

people. Likewise, it should be remembered that this description is by way of an introduction—general background material for the more detailed accounts that follow, in which specific shades of categorization will be explicated, as reflected in various social activities and as shaped by them.

Kleenier (1961, 286) distinguishes between three social frameworks in which the elderly find themselves: their community, including their family and neighbors; their age group—elderly people like themselves; and the institution. In the old-age home researched there is a partial congruence of the two latter frameworks, for the residents' activities within the home are carried out in many cases with age-peers—although this is not necessarily so—and in addition to their contacts with staff they receive visitors (not just family) and thus the community framework penetrates into the home. Moreover, some residents maintain contacts outside the home with other elderly people, such as clubs for the elderly in which they participated prior to admission to the home. It is useful then to speak of three systems of social relations to which the residents are party: contacts with the staff, relations with other residents, and meetings with "outsiders" such as family, friends, and representatives of organizations.

The description presented below is based on the following claim: departure from the institution as a result of functional deterioration carries with it a fear of death. Therefore, residents develop a tendency to set up cognitive and physical barriers between themselves and other residents who represent this possibility. At the same time, leaving the home in order to return to their former world with its ties and identities is not really possible, a situation finding expression in a feeling of abject rejection by that world. Thus, the institutional environment remains the only field of action in which patterns of behavior and categories from the outside are adopted in order to differentiate between residents, despite the fact that these categories are actually systems of symbols with no direct relevance to what occurs in the home. The static enclave created as a result of this complex of factors provides a basis for the crystallization of perceptions of dependence on the staff and on the social networks outside the institution on the one hand, and on the other, of the existence of intra-institutional attempts to construct alternative worlds of content that include within them the possibility of building up and giving meaning to an unchanging reality. This chapter will include a general description of the cognitive background supporting this set of arguments.

I

Leaving the home is perceived by the residents as the start of an inevitable process of deterioration, culminating in death. Most of the residents are aware that their days are numbered. This consciousness is exacerbated by the threatening warning signs of sickness and difficulties in functioning that they are bound to experience at times. Death seems close both cognitively—in the self-perception of the residents—and also physically—in the condition of those residents who seem to be on its threshold. How does one cope with that fine division between inside and out; that is to say, between life and death? How does it show itself in the social reality of the home?

In the home studied, the incidence of death is no greater than in other old-age homes, and from this standpoint there was no direct, public confrontation with death. At the same time, it cannot be claimed that the preoccupation with thoughts about death and the associated attitude toward it is the same for residents of such homes and the noninstitutionalized elderly. A number of features of institutional life impose a certain singularity of mind towards death. The activism preached by the management and channelled into appropriate "functioning" does not make for open discussions about death. All the organized activities in the home are of a kind that provide the possibility of attainable goals in a reasonably short span of time. With respect to the ordinary daily, voluntary activities of the residents (in the office, sick rooms, dining room, and laundry), they seem to undertake only short-term actions, sometimes requiring just several minutes, and not involving any long-term programs. In the case of group activity, the situation is different, and in some cases plans for the attainment of a specific goal are made for a period up to a year (the "work" group for instance). However, here also, the goal is subdivided into short-term targets, attainable without regard to the ultimate goal (the making of various articles). The selfsame people who spoke openly about the likelihood of their own demise and of the feeling of depression or relief accompanying these thoughts were the less active and more socially isolated residents

26

who did not want to stay in the home at any price—not even at the price of "good functioning."

Transfer to the infirmary provides a kind of preparation for the onset of death for the sick resident, since in many cases she does not return to her bedroom. Visits to the sickrooms are few, and the residents tend to keep away from the vicinity of the sick wing. The creation of a physical barrier is in turn reinforced by barriers of a verbal nature as well as social stratification. When a resident dies, it is not customary to mention his or her name, and even if this taboo is broken, it is generally emphasized that life goes on, despite the passing, which is perceived as a melancholy event. After the death of one of the most loved and admired of the residents, I encountered a marked reluctance to acknowledge the fact of his passing and its effect on the other residents. Generally, individuals related to the subject with sentences like: "It's too bad he died, but life goes on." This was emphasized when some residents went so far as to stress that the fact of the man's death would not be allowed to interfere with the programs of the groups in which he had been active, and that they would continue to operate without him.

This barrier to the acknowledgement of death is even more striking when seen against the residents' perception of the stratified structure of the home. At the top of the ladder are the active and healthy in mind and body. At the bottom are the elderly whose poor physical condition, relative to others, is such as to impair their free-dom of movement and whose verbal reactions are limited and usu-ally not intelligible. There is no way of knowing whether these resi-dents have descended into an inner sanctum that insulates them against the external world, or whether this behavior is a result of psychological processes over which they have no control. It is even possible that a reciprocal relationship exists between the two alter-natives. At any rate, this category imparts to the place the aura of an old-age home, with a feeling of depression encompassing those entering it. The active residents are aware and sensitive to this effect and the implications it has for the home's general image, a fact that increases their resentment and disgust at the presence of these individuals.

Ironically, perhaps, it may be said that were it not for their presence, the other residents would not have the material with which to erect the physical/cognitive barrier between themselves and death. It is the very gulf, as perceived between those individuals

27

and the others, that emphasizes their different identities. It is expressed in the linguistic labels attached to them by the residents, labels whose significance lies beyond their simple definition. There are three nicknames applied to these individuals: "exhibition," "vegetables," and "animals." These three nicknames exclude those so designated from any human frame of reference.[2] Since these residents are the most likely candidates for transfer, and later for an early death, the creation of this nonhuman category[3] itself serves as a barrier both against death and also against the possibility of removal from the home. As long as the resident defines themself in human terms and their neighbor as nonhuman, the gap between the two by its very nature will be unbridgeable. Therefore, the possibility that the same resident will reach that stage can be rejected.[4] In the application of this social strategy, a form of a social death sentence[5] is passed on these people before they actually die. This social death excludes them from the world of the living, abrogates their rights, and justifies an inhumane attitude toward them. At the same time, while there is ordinarily an ambivalent attitude toward corpses that accords them some vestige of life, here their diminution to the status of objects is total and uncompromising. Any attempt to humanize these residents with any of the accoutrements of the living would mean breaking down the barrier.

The rejection of the "vegetables" in the structuring of the residents' world as a static, unchanging enclave may be exemplified by staff attitudes toward the phenomenon. On more than one occasion, the staff have expressed surprise at this mode of evaluation, asking whether "the selfsame elderly individual who relates to his peers thus and will find himself tomorrow in the same state, is really aware of the fact?" Apparently, this is the function of the categorization—to prevent the possibility of awareness of this fact, to remove it from the individual's private world as far as possible, and through the social endorsement of this view to strengthen the creation of this barrier.

The approach to death is not the only feature delineating the environment outside the home from the internal reality. Additional forces and factors exist that the residents see as a threat to their self-image and as a danger to the comparative security in which they find themselves.

Many residents view the attitude of the nonaged world towards them as rejecting, and in some cases even mocking, contemptuous, and scornful. As a result, considerable reservation and suspicion have developed in the institution toward uninvited guests who are not counted as family or friends known to the resident. Thus, for example, residents can be seen going over to the inquiry desk, in order to report on the presence of a stranger in the place. Some incidents of theft from the bedrooms strengthened this attitude and exacerbated the feelings of powerlessness of many residents. The derision displayed by the young, and especially by children towards old people,[6] provided a common topic of conversation and a forum for self-expression for the residents. In addition, there were indications that this problem was perhaps the main impetus bringing them into the home in the first place, and that it was also the cause of their reluctance to venture outside to any great extent. One incident that made a deep impression on the residents and that reinforced in many their alienation from the world outside was when a gang of youths pestered two female residents on their way to the home, and beat them up severely (enough to cause some fractures) while cursing and jeering at them. No overt motive for the attack was revealed. Many residents were unable to prevent themselves from discussing the incident for a considerable length of time, and for a large number of them it served as an endorsement of their view of society's negative attitude towards them. This leads to an ambivalent attitude toward children and young people, one of the problems with which many old people try to come to terms. Their strong attachments to their children—and especially their grandchildren—as the recipients of affection, rights, and family ties on the one hand, and the negative attitude of young people towards the "rejected" aged on the other, create a basic contradiction in their perception of the world.

This ambivalent attitude is interwoven in the references of many residents to members of their family and informs their contacts with them. The sense of being "cut off" and of an enveloping depression lays heavily on the old people who were forced to give up their homes for an institution and is seen in the lack of enthusiasm to discuss family ties, particularly the relationship with their children. At the same time, complete estrangement is not contemplated and only a few hinted that they would prefer to sever completely the loose and painful ties with their children. A cursory follow-up of the behavioral indicators of the links between residents and their children reveals their paucity and irregularity. The telephone booths in the building, for example, are never crowded with residents trying to contact their children and there is also no demand for telephones with outside lines in the rooms. Visits to family are few and far between, and reciprocal visits from the family to the home usually occur in the early evening and last only a short time. It is a rare occurrence to find a group of family members gathered together on the lawn or ensconced in the bedroom of their parents for a special occasion.

The subjects of the conversations on these visits usually do not extend beyond such routine matters as health, general satisfaction, and an "update" on what is happening within the family circle. I cannot recall cases of common recollections from a shared past ever being aired, or of any discussions of controversial content such as bringing up children, or future plans, and so on. Conspicuously absent from these conversations were subjects such as the meaning of life in an old-age home, family separation, and relations with the staff and other residents. There was a discernable desire to restrict the conversational content of the visits to a level that would not arouse tension. The reason for this seems to reside in the consciousness of the aged that changed family relations are not reversible and that being in an old-age home has transformed them, via a shift into a different existential dimension from that of the past and into one in which the resident finds themself subject to a pervasive set of daily relations in which they fulfill a secondary and marginal role.

Support for this view can be found in the fact that most of the residents are not financially dependent on their families. The low monthly maintenance charge and the one-time admission deposit are within the financial grasp of almost every old person (from savings, pensions, sale of property, etc.), especially since the residents in this particular old-age home come from a comparatively well-off economic background. This is yet another reason why the residents are afraid of a change in their condition that might facilitate their removal. Such a change would cause them to become a burden on their families and create a new dependency that both sides wish to avoid. In general, one gets the impression that the residents do not derive much satisfaction from family visits, one party seeing them as an obligation, and the other not exactly relishing the fact.[7]

II

Family members and other visitors to the institution also provide internal symbols of respect that help define the interrelations among the residents themselves. This is a wholly different function from that usually attributed to the ties between the aged and their nonaged social environment; that is, respite from loneliness and an enrichment of the content of their social life. The presence of visitors in the home provides a recognizable indication of the relations of a resident with the outside world, and, as has been intimated, the stronger these ties are the more they raise the status of the resident in the eyes of the staff and the other residents. An old person receiving many visits is seen as the beneficiary of a free choice rather than as the victim of his family's desire to be rid of him as far as his being in the home is concerned, all the more so since his relatives seek his company even when he is ensconced in the home. So one can witness residents receiving their guests and visitors in the entrance hall or in the garden surrounding the home, even when the former is crowded and the weather unsuitable for the latter. Many residents inform their peers about some "bigwig" or other who comes to visit them, and thus famous names become a status symbol among the old people. Other visitors whose presence confers prestige on their hosts are young people considered successful in the wider society. One female resident, a retired teacher, is prone to tell of the visits of her former pupils, concentrating, however, on the most successful, particularly those who have distinguished themselves in the world of art. Another way of demonstrating ties with the outside world is through group photographs with family or friends. Such photographs are passed around, with the number of people appearing in the picture and their public prominence providing a yardstick for determining the possessor's status in the world outside the old-age home. It must be stressed here that we are not dealing with a nostalgic preoccupation with or absorption in an extant past, but with a reinforcement of the present.[8]

The exchange of photographs with accompanying explanations is only one of the ways available for the symbolic transfer of information, whose source is to be found outside the institution, from one resident to another. Other symbols current in the home, serving to denote the residents' status both outside and within the home, are of several kinds, and for purposes of illustration we will cite two of them. The modes of dress of the residents are of three sorts—this, according to their own classification: "dandified," "modest," and "sloppy." Suits, expensive dresses, and jewelry are not taken as signs of personal vanity, but as belonging to a defined group of residents who feel themselves isolated from the others—those com-

31

ing from English-speaking countries. Some of them have already discarded their accustomed dress for what they consider to be "Israeli" attire. The "Israeli look" characterizes those who see themselves and are seen by others as belonging to the local "elite," comprised mainly of elderly individuals who were active in the Histadrut or in any other public institutions and who define their own dress as "modest." In contrast to this, "sloppy" clothing is characteristic of the "vegetables"—those old people who do not indulge in any sort of activity and whose neglected appearance is apparently part of their general image. These three types of mode of dress are only part of a complex of symbols attesting to the differences between the residents and in contrast with existing symbols whose significance outside the institution helps to distinguish between individuals but are of no importance within the home. For example, money. The residents in the home (or their families) are elderly individuals who can afford to pay the maintenance costs demanded. But since the sum involved is the same for all, at least formally, money is not a decisive factor and its importance is negligible.

The restriction imposed on keeping private items in the rooms and the low evaluation placed on expensive clothing are conducive to the creation of this situation. Consequently, "resident power" is not dependent on financial resources, but rather on a variety of other variables that will be discussed later—mainly ties with the outside world and activity within the home. Another symbol denoting significant differences between residents is the use of the Hebrew language. Older people in Israel use Hebrew less (Bachi 1971) and rely more on foreign tongues, such as Yiddish and Ladino. This is indeed part of the negative stereotype of the elderly in Israel. Lack of fluency in Hebrew, or even a foreign accent and speech patterns different from the norm, are seen as symptomatic behaviors that place the old person at the bottom of the social ladder. The emphasis on the fluent use of Hebrew in the home gives those who possess this facility a critical resource in their social relations. It is a boundary for social acceptance or rejection that is very difficult to manipulate, and generally speaking, the correlation between it and other characteristics of the resident, such as length of time in Israel, ties with public organizations and institutions, and so on, is clear and direct. Paradoxically, it is just because other components of status have disappeared or have been eroded that fluency in Hebrew has been transformed from a mere reflection of other variables into an autonomous stratifying factor. It is one of the important elements in the structuring of reality of the residents, where a symbolic code has been taken out of its daily context and serves as an intra-institutional stratification device.

This is expressed principally in the mode of expression of Hebrew—"good" Hebrew, with correct syntax and polished sentences. Here, too, the removal of the code from its context has brought about the employment of language exceeding the bounds of ordinary everyday usage, which is not generally characterized by such qualities. So, for instance, the use of sophisticated Hebrew is appreciated, in contrast to the rather stilted reaction it would arouse outside the institution, even in circles where such sophistication is commonplace.

There are many examples of this phenomenon. The most common language spoken in the institution is Yiddish, but when residents who are not acquainted try to approach each other they tend to employ Hebrew. In public places, residents fluent in both languages opt for Hebrew and when a member of the "discussion group" (see below) or someone identified with this group is circulating, this tendency is even more in evidence. In one case, two women residents were standing outside the clinic entrance chatting away in Yiddish about, not unexpectedly, medical matters. However, when the subject turned to a fellow woman resident, a leading protagonist in the discussion group and noted for her fluent Hebrew, the two suddenly switched from Yiddish to Hebrew. In this case, the context determined the language used, possibly not altogether consciously.

Another instance of the importance of language is in the setting up of Hebrew study groups at various levels, the lively participation in these groups, and the publicity accorded them by the residents themselves. Two reasons can be advanced to explain the phenomenon. Correct use of language generally provides a clear indication of a "functioning" or "good" old person (in the residents' own jargon). The reaction of an old person to a question thrown at her, her ability to hold a conversation, and to involve herself in any kind of activity within the Home, depends on her verbal facility. Unclear speech, accompanied by a stream of unfathomable associations, points to someone who is not in control of her actions and is incapable of playing her part in the orderly institutional routine.

Why then Hebrew? The answer is to be found in the kind of resident most admired in the home. These individuals are well versed in public speaking in general, and in manipulating Hebrew in particular, and thus the polished use of Hebrew has become a pivotal symbol in the home. Of course, this ability was not acquired in the home but rather "imported" by those residents who developed this facility by way of their outside activities.

Manipulation of and control over Hebrew as a symbol of social differentiation is connected with the way in which the outside world penetrates the institution. It must be remembered that, ostensibly, the residents are exposed continuously to the outside media of communication through newspapers, etc., and in contrast to Townsend's findings (1961, 296–313) they do not have to prepare meals, shop, or worry about cleaning, so that, from the standpoint of the amount of time at their disposal, and the permeation of media material, they are able to absorb a considerable amount of news from the outside. The television sets and radios found in almost every room enable recreation to be enjoyed individually and in select groups within the rooms. Not all residents are able to enjoy television programs. A great number have impaired eyesight and find it hard to concentrate for any length of time, particularly since for some programs it is necessary to follow the Hebrew subtitles. These difficulties also affect the reading of newspapers and books. The amount of borrowing from the library is minimal and the home has had to refuse the offers of various groups to donate books. A daily newspaper is to be found in many rooms, but not a few residents complain that they cannot get through the whole paper, and confine themselves to perusal of the headlines only. Reading a newspaper has become in the home one of the indices of self-estimation for the resident and of evaluation by their fellows. Readers of *Davar*,[9] for instance, are identified with the discussion group, and so many residents subscribe to it although they may prefer a foreign newspaper. Sometimes a resident complains to the manager and to his neighbors that his newspaper has been stolen from his mailbox, demonstrating perhaps more than the desire to have his pilfered newspaper returned, than that he is an enthusiastic and interested reader.

Speaking Hebrew and reading Hebrew newspapers are not the only labels of identification advertising the stratification code within the home. Public announcements of concertgoing, visits to the theater, participation in lectures and different courses of study, etc., also attest to the membership of a select group of residents who are identified as having strong ties with the world outside the institution. On the other hand, worshipping in a synagogue outside the institution or membership in any external religious circle are not status-enhancing pursuits. One resident agreed to tell me, but only after much hesitation, that he was active in a religious study group outside the home. Within the home itself, cultural activities such as concerts, plays, films and lectures are staged periodically. (All this in addition to the routine activities of the various interest groups, which will be described later.) But the residents do not regard these activities as especially conducive to social or self-esteem. Possibly the reason for this is to be found in the difficulties associated with participation in similar activities outside the home (from the standpoint of physical mobility). But it seems more likely that this differentiation stems from the awareness that whoever participates in activities of this type (outside the home) belongs to groups and organizations by virtue of his social gifts rather than (and perhaps in spite of) his being a resident of an old-age home.

III

These issues find succinct and comprehensive expression in the residents' own newsletter *Dvar Ha'avot*,[10] a venture encouraged by the management. The articles, stories, letters, puzzles, and poems that are published monthly in the publication and edited by the discussion group team must be submitted in Hebrew. An analysis of a number of topics chosen and the mode of presentation are instructive regarding some additional aspects of the residents' lives and their ties with the reality that lies outside the bounds of the home.[11]

   Goffman (1961a, 95–96) proposes looking upon the newspaper of a total institution as a sort of ritual accessory containing censored news from the outside and as explanatory material set forth by the staff to the inmates reflecting its "ideal" approach to them. So it appears likely that an analysis of the subjects in *Dvar Ha'avot* may reveal something about those issues that are of pivotal importance in the old people's world. It is also clear that the state of staff-resident relations is reflected in the newspaper, but this is peripheral. We shall investigate the main types of subject matter, but first we shall survey the accepted modes of expression in the newsletter.

Most of the written material is in the form of articles, while some is expressed by way of quotation (for example, a comment on the significance of Independence Day). Letters also have a niche in the publication (mainly correspondence of the management and the discussion group with individuals and institutions outside the old-age home). Another genre is the poem—simply constructed rhyming poems with a largely moral content; some description of nature, but mainly alluding to old age. In the same vein, proverbs and original epigrams, even jokes, are represented. Some jokes allude to some of the central issues encountered by the residents. For example: "Residents who come back late at night are requested not to make a lot of noise so as not to disturb the night watchman's sleep," or "The table-setters, especially those responsible for the fruit, are requested to measure precisely the dimensions of each piece of fruit with the aid of a slide rule in order to prevent quarrels breaking out amongst the diners."

The topics dealt with in the written material can be classified according to the following central issues:

Quantitatively, most space is devoted to references to holidays and festivals following within the period of issue. Quotations from original sources along with surveys of the festival's customs and its importance make up the largest part of this kind of material. Independence Day has a special place and more is made of it than of any other festival. The character of the material, by virtue of its national-historical aspects, dovetails with the material devoted to other holidays (articles on the evaluation of Passover as a national holiday, the heroism of the Maccabees, etc.). However, greatest prominence was given to the articles dealing with Jewish history— of which there are many—to the subject of Aliyah (immigration) to Israel, incidents from the War of Independence, the blood libels and other anti-Semitic manifestations, the Holocaust, and so on. The newspaper covered all these subjects. Personal memoirs are also accorded honorable status in the pages of *Dvar Ha'avot*, most of them imbued with a strong nationalistic tone, finding expression sometimes in declarations such as: "I always had the country in mind." Other foci for recollections are the earliest days of the country, the yearning for the Land of Israel, and its settlement (for instance, a piece on Yemenite immigration). One article carrying the title: "A Personal Biography," tells the story of one family by means

36

of its members' attempts to reach Israel. Another article tells of the writer's meeting with Ben-Gurion,[12] and yet a third relates to how the Italians helped the writer's family during Fascist rule.

All these examples show the writers' attempts to imbue the present reality of the home with something of their past. This "instillment" is undertaken, among other reasons, in order to emphasize their bonds with important personalities in the country and their activities on behalf of the "Yishuv"[13] and their place in it. Since most of the contributors to the paper are members of the discussion group, there appears to be a double purpose attached to this kind of writing: the creation of a standard of evaluation within the home based on the place of the writers outside it, together with a sort of covert competition among themselves according to the same ground rules.

Another subject preoccupying the paper's contributors is old age. Old age is typically described as a phenomenon from which there is no escape, but one which can and must be overcome. One article blames society itself for the material and social condition of old people, and cites instances of famous people who achieved a full expression of potential in their senescence. Another article on this subject is in the form of a letter to an anonymous friend in which the writer praises the home as an appropriate residential setting for the old (in terms of the unexacting time scale, humanity, the approach of the staff, etc.). The least-discussed subject reflected in the pages of the newsletter (although quantitatively it is one of the most meaningful) is that of relations with the staff. There are two aspects to this topic: what is written by members of the staff to the residents and what is written by the residents about the staff in return. The staff address the residents on different issues, such as expressions of thanks for cooperation, a speech made by the manager in which he praises the activities of the residents' working groups, and the manager's letters to outside bodies together with their replies. (It should be understood that the newspaper is also distributed to other Mishan old-age homes and to different bodies extending services to the elderly or to the home studied.) For our purposes the communication initiated by the residents to the staff is more important. Complimentary pieces on one or another member of the staff can be found (usually the manager), but words of criticism are also expressed directly, by implication, or through the medium of a joke (see the

37

example below). The Purim[14] issue abounded with such "barbs" which allude to some of the "sores" troubling the residents, for example:[15]

PURIM GIFTS

To the manager of Mishan:

I hope he will get rich quick from the (latest) round of price increases inflicted on us.

To our manager:

Thanks for the 'sermon' he bestows on us every morning which makes us feel like kindergarten kids (at best) or even nursery-school tots.

To one of the kitchen staff:

Let's hope salt will go up in price so you won't be able to use so much of it in the soup and in other dishes.

To another kitchen hand:

Get well soon so you can give us the pleasure of eating your good cakes instead of the biscuits we can't even stand to look at anymore.

PURIM GIFTS TO OUR MANAGER

First, I want him to partake of a quiet and relaxed breakfast, but this is only possible on the condition that he is not assailed early in the morning as soon as he reaches his office with shouts of: Mr. Manager, they've 'knocked off' my newspaper again,[16] etc.

In addition I wish him luck in installing the new telephones in the corridors, so that they are not stolen and the tables under them removed . . . I also hope that during his room visits, he will not find, God forbid, an electric kettle or any other electrical appliance[17] . . . he will find the rooms tidy, clean and even aesthetically pleasing to his eye and that the corridors and lifts will not be strewn with scraps of paper, fruit peels, milk and yogurt stains, etc., etc. I would hope that there will be no more quarrels or the occasional exchange of blows between roommates, since this would undoubtedly give him a great deal of pleasure, as would the willingness of some actor or singer to give us a free show, or an interesting lecture or even an Army concert—can I wish him more than that?

I would like to add to my greetings at least a few Purim cakes, but since the Manager does not accept any gifts, I will confine myself to wishing him a happy life.

The final quips relating in some measure to staff-resident relations bring us to the last topic connected with the organization of life in the home. This is the type of behavior Goffman calls "underlife" (1961a). While associated with overt and public behavior, the concept of the underlife assumes an important place as a background to these public behaviors, as one of the subjects connected to this question. Moreover, staff-resident relations are not uniform, and thus there is always an element of uncertainty and insecurity in social relations within the institution.

The staff's attitude is complex and varies according to the staff member's expertise in dealing with old people, his personality, and the situations in which he finds himself in his contacts with the residents. Generally speaking, the professional staff abstain from giving or receiving personal gifts, but the attitude of the nonprofessional staff is ambivalent; on the one hand, extremely bitter sentiments towards the elderly come to the fore, sometimes culminating in an exchange of blows, after comments such as: "You're not human," "Tomorrow you may all die," or "When I reach sixty, I'd rather kill myself than end up like all of you." On the other hand, and also characteristic of their approach, it was precisely these individuals who were inclined to receive gifts in exchange to undertake special duties such as more efficient cleaning of rooms, serving of particular kinds of food, and so on. The explanation seems to lie not in the interpersonal distance between the resident and the nonprofessional staff member (for as we have seen there is strong antipathy towards the old people), but rather in the kind of bond between them

39

which, by its very nature, is specific to a certain defined purpose and usually short-lived, for there is a high turnover of such staff in the home. Giving presents (money or its equivalent in modest amounts) to this category of staff does not complicate the resident's relations with other individuals (for these workers enjoy only loose ties with the permanent staff) and does not lead to any deterioration in relations with the particular individual. These relations are one-dimensional and offering a gift is not likely to affect other aspects of the relationship with the staff worker. In other words, the close and direct form of contact created between resident and staff member, its one-dimensional nature, and the fact that these individuals (staff) are responsible for the provision of basic material conditions in the home, create opportunities and possibilities for the exchange of gifts for services rendered.

Many avenues are open to the resident to draw attention to herself and to demonstrate her own individuality within the total institution by infringing upon its rules, appearing sloppily dressed, trying to impress by means of a bogus erudition, eccentric behavior, etc.[18] One phenomenon serving this end is the imagined theft. Residents declare that some valuable article has been stolen from them (radio transistor, watch, etc.) and request the manager's help in finding the culprit. The manager knows from experience the unreliability of many of these demands, and therefore does not even bother to look for the "thief." The resident himself is not really interested in discovering the culprit but rather more in drawing attention to himself and, even more than this, of attaining social and personal recognition of his importance. The fact that he was robbed makes him, in his own eyes, a person occupying "center stage" for a short time, and as someone of whom notice is taken, even if this is expressed (negatively) in the act of theft. It is possible that the desire to demonstrate ownership of certain personal items also influences this phenomenon. Another device calculated to gain the attention of the management and in some cases even contriving to operate as a source of power, is the phenomenon of "squealing" to the manager. Many residents do not hesitate to approach the manager and to tell him about what they know—and sometimes even what they imagine—about their comrades. Despite the reservations of the manager regarding this practice as a source of information, he will sometimes make use of it (a detailed incident of this kind will be described in the chapter on the occupational therapy group).

40

IV

Although the home provides an all-embracing living framework, which creates conditions against which the residents react, this system is really built up through reciprocal contact between staff and residents vis-à-vis the wider society. This means that what happens within the home can be seen as the totality of these behaviors, accompanied by feedback. This dynamic aspect of life in the home finds its expression on a number of levels.

The residents receive in the old-age home material services that more or less approximate those that existed at home. Similarly, they also develop personal ties furnishing them with a form of community in which they act out their daily lives. Despite this, not all of the residents consider the place as their home.[19] Some relate to it as though it were a hotel or a pension (witness the Mrs. Tsefrani affair below). Others discover in the home a medium for wide-ranging social pursuits. These different ways of regarding the home are connected with distinctive patterns of activity among the resident population. While a few of them consider the home to be the pivot of their personal and social world, as well as that of the outside world, set in a framework of greater or lesser meaningfulness, other residents conversely see their contacts with the outside world as their focus of activity and identification, thus minimizing their interest in other residents. It is conceivable that the lack of uniformity between these different levels of reference constitutes one of the causes for the creation of a system of categories that are incongruous, based on symbolic codes, different and even contradictory at times.

The combination of different frameworks of reference with the structural characteristics of the institution, seen against the backdrop of the general problems associated with old age, brings us to consider the existence of multiple worlds of meanings that are disharmonious and unsynchronized. Time is static but it changes; death is close but more remote than ever; symbols of identity and stratification shape institutional life, in some ways more than ever before, but they do not rest upon the same systems the individual's personal and social identity previously belonged to in the past; the staff are necessary, but create dependence and stigmatization; the family exists but kinship ties undergo transformation. All these paradoxes engender a disorganized, amorphous view of the world.

The next chapter will describe how this picture of the world organizes itself through the channels of communication between the staff and residents, or more precisely, through the ability and efforts of the residents to control their own fates.

3. FIELDS OF CONTROL

The organization of life in the home should not be viewed in terms of a rigid framework of predetermined activities, based on a fixed daily schedule and other constants the old people are obliged to accept. Rather, the model informing the description and analysis to follow is one of constant negotiation of social images and their control (Strauss et al., 1963). This examination will be conducted by further study of the various aspects of the concept of "functioning," which constitutes the very heart of the power and dependency relationships between the residents and the management. Moreover, this concept represents the central axis around which the lives of the residents revolve, as well as the principle expression of one of their most pressing existential difficulties—resistance to change.

It is possible to understand the arguments and conflicts surrounding the definition of functioning simply in terms of power, whose function is to provide a definition of the situation convenient for one of the parties. At the same time, however, it is hard to appreciate the importance attached to the matter and its concomitant implications without taking into consideration the wider meaning of functioning in the evolution of the old person's self-image and in its operation as a symbolic code denoting the individual's struggle against change. The analysis presented below will concern itself with a description of the problem of functioning, set against the background of the various fields of power in the home. First, I will focus on the sources of the manager's power in his dealings with the staff, since I claim his control over them imbues him with a special and exclusive standing in his relations with the residents. Explicating the various aspects entailed in the definition of functioning as a key for understanding the relations between the manager and the residents, I will show how this works in the home. Finally, the chapter concludes with a survey of the factors shaping the various fields of control within the institution and the ties between them and the fields of relevance embraced by the residents, as described in the previous chapter.

/

The manager's power derives from two sources and his influence draws from their successful operation and the relationship between them.

1) Control over the admission and removal of residents—his notion of what constitutes "functioning"—is a source of power bestowed on him by an external factor: Mishan.
2) Financial resources—complete control of the budget with the possibility of increasing it (via his connections within the Mishan directorate, but mainly by virtue of the home's prestigious status and the residents' political connection.

These two factors are not automatic or invulnerable to change, and the manager must devote some of his energies toward maintaining and strengthening them. Before detailing these sources of power and their implications, it should be stressed that while the manager enjoys them by virtue of his being a Mishan man, he nevertheless makes a considerable effort to extend his contacts and activities within the Histadrut, among other areas, as insurance in order to ensure a firm basis for his continued influence in case certain contacts cannot be exploited. For example, his contacts with the secretary-general of the Histadrut were made in order to propose a selective and graduated retirement plan for Histadrut members. In addition, he tries to establish ties with bodies outside the Histadrut, in order to provide an alternative for himself should his standing with Mishan be threatened. He tries to foster contacts with a nearby university, as well as with the Israeli Gerontological Association and other private agencies, in the hope that "scientific research will corroborate the correctness of his approach to the treatment for the aged." He made a point of stressing that he had job offers from these institutions, and that he was staying with Mishan because of the free hand he enjoyed in running the home. To these bodies, he tries to present a position that justifies the special features of his institution ("a homogeneous institution") by recourse to a variety of different arguments. Principally, he maintains that a home of this type is able to mobilize a great deal of organizational and financial effort in activating the residents both socially and occupationally. Thus, the manager furnishes an index of success for himself as manager of the

44

home. This stance is rooted in the fear that the home will gradually be transformed into a heterogeneous institution; that is, a home that incorporates different kinds of residents—fully functioning, as well as those not functioning at all. It can be assumed that in a home such as this the concept of functioning will take on a completely different complexion. In such a set of circumstances, a manager would not be able to continue to carry out his functions as he does today. The increase in the complement of medical staff and their consequent elevation in importance in the home would lead to the appointment of a "medical" professional as manager, or at least would afford him a great measure of authority and control over resources, as in heterogeneous institutions. The desire to prove the success of his approach finds expression in his efforts to set up groups of various sorts that serve as frameworks for social activity in the home.

In order to realize this policy, the manager needs to optimally concentrate the resources in the institution, both in order to ensure a great deal of flexibility in his relations with the residents—upon which the determination of functioning is dependent—and also in the assertion of firm control of those staff who might undermine the achievement of his goal. What then is the constellation of factors that the manager has at his disposal and that he can exploit in order to achieve the aims described above?

I do not have either reliable or accurate information on the financial resources at the home's disposal, but it is possible to obtain data on the ways money is used and its implications for what transpires there. The administration of the home's financial transactions is in the hands of the manager and he does not allow anyone else to utilize the home's funds. There are many examples of this. For instance, the purchase of a spool of scotch tape (IL 1.60; about 1$) was personally approved by the manager and he even handed over the money needed for the purchase. When the employee, who had requested the purchase, returned and told the manager that the spool actually cost twenty agorot more (about 13 cents) the extra cash was then provided. At the same time, the manager was negotiating with a supplier over a purchase amounting to several thousand lirot. Even the female office staff are not authorized to pay out any money without permission. The same also applies to service personnel. A kitchen worker found himself obliged to request extra funds for the purchase of choice biscuits. That the manager does not skimp on

45

purchases of good quality food products the residents agree, but no service employee is able to effect a purchase independently. This control of the "purse strings" enables the manager to exert a direct influence over both staff employment and on the level of material living conditions in the home, with their resultant effects on the lives of the residents. We will now enlarge on these points.

The staff in the home consists of about fifty people, largely unskilled and temporary workers. Some see their work as a secondary source of income for a limited period (students), while others are looking for a more lucrative source of livelihood and leave the home on finding it. The manager is in contact with the local Labor Exchange, but complains of difficulties in getting the right kind of help. At the same time he refuses to grant wage increases and fringe benefits that might dissuade workers from leaving. The situation suits the manager—for as long as he is able to supply the necessary basic services for the home—since he does not need to pay the same wage to established and organized workers with seniority. The system of direct payment to the employee creates the possibility of individual negotiation with the manager, but not on the group level. In this way the establishment of a workers' committee that might exert pressure for a general wage increase is averted. On the eve of the Jewish New Year, one of the kitchen staff came to the manager's office, wished him a happy New Year, and in a roundabout manner asked for a raise. The manager countered that in his opinion her existing wage met her needs and that her work did not justify an increase. When the woman continued to press her case, he asked her to leave and not to bother him any further. It can be assumed that if the employee had tried to wrest an increase in wages operating within some sort of organized framework embracing the home's employees, the possibility of a favorable outcome for her request would have been enhanced.

The real threat to the curbing of the manager's absolute power emanates from the permanent, professional staff, which, as has been mentioned, is very small and comprises a doctor working half-time (50 percent), a nurse, a chief nursing auxiliary, chef, a housemother, and the superintendent responsible for the upkeep of the home. There are additional professional auxiliary staff in the home, but they are subject to frequent turnover.

The manager fears that increased professionalization will create the conditions necessary for transforming the home into a heterogeneous institution, in which his powers will be significantly reduced. This danger is a real one, because of the severe shortage of space for the bedridden elderly—and the great pressures arising from this—as well as the fact that the home is well equipped for such a transition.

How then is the manager's power safeguarded? A number of factors account for this: the coordinator of the nursing auxiliary staff, the nurse, and the superintendent (who is incidentally married to the nurse) were brought in by the manager from the home in which he previously worked (Malben) and they are resident just as he is, a situation that partially explains their trepidation in wanting to quarrel with him, especially since they can formulate their own schedules and are effectively given a free rein. Close cooperation between them is readily discernable, finding expression in mutual assistance, and in their approaches toward the residents (this matter will be clarified in the consideration of the discussion group). Both the fact of their joint living quarters and the freedom they enjoy create considerable mutual dependency between them and the manager.

Another factor that allows the manager to continue exercising power lies in the homogeneous nature of the home; that is, there is no ostensible reason for employing many medical or heavy nursing staff. More than once the manager mentions that a 380-bed geriatric center is being built to which the infirm elderly will be sent. That is his stock reply to the question of why he does not employ a larger medical staff complement in the home, even though it is not known with any certainty when the building of the center will commence. The argument for not employing a social worker on the permanent staff, who could visit applicants in their homes and determine their degree of functioning is, he maintains, financial. "No budget," he declares, and claims that the services provided by the housemother and the head social worker of Mishan (who visits occasionally) for the treatment of the social problems within the home are adequate. Even the services of the latter were received grudgingly by the manager, with continuous attempts to restrict her activities and possibilities of action among the residents, mainly because the manager assumes the functions she is supposed to perform and thus drains her job of meaningful content.

The refusal to increase the professional staff complement is most obvious in the manager's dealings with the doctor. As previously mentioned, there is a doctor on the premises who is employed half-time. Thus, long queues frequently form outside his surgery door and many residents prefer to receive medical treatment from the local Kupat Holim clinic to which they belonged prior to their admission to the home. I know of cases in which residents elected to forego lunch in the home and travelled on several buses in order to reach their former clinic—all this to avoid having to stand in line for the home's doctor. To those residents who complain about the quality of the medical services, the manager replies that he has no budget at his disposal and that the Mishan headquarters refuses to authorize an allocation for a full-time doctor. However, the manager admitted to me that he could get almost any kind of allocation for the home. Corroboration may be found in the fact that this home is considered a Mishan showpiece and attracts many visitors and guests. Since there is no chance that the house doctor can satisfy all the demands made on him for treatment and the residents might convey their disgruntlement to the "higher authorities"—and there are those with such power and connections—the manager sometimes employs a specialist in gerontological medicine, one of the top men in the country in this field, who performs examinations and prescribes treatment for selected residents in the afternoon. Every consultation of this kind is very expensive, but it does allow the manager to solve the problem of a lack of suitable medical care without damaging his authority within the home, or his good name outside it. Expanding the medical staff might gradually take out of the manager's hands the determination of what constitutes functioning and with it the final say on the removal of residents. The employment of an outside specialist obviates this danger, and increases the dependence of the residents on the manager, who acts as an intermediary for them with the specialist, while direct contact with the house doctor continues as before.

To illustrate this state of affairs I will relate two incidents that highlight the tense relationship between the house doctor and the manager set against the background of the demand for increasing the medical complement. One day around noon, the doctor burst into the manager's office, which is connected to his own, and complained bitterly about his enormous work load, with which he was unable to cope. He demanded either extending his working hours or hiring an additional physician. The manager replied that he sympathized with him and that he was trying to secure an extra half-time job allocation from Mishan, but that he did not have the budget for it. On another occasion, after finishing his day's work, the doctor came into the manager's office and told him that there was a danger of an outbreak of intestinal infection among the residents. The manager refused to accept this warning, professing confidence in the quality of the food products purchased for the home. On hearing this defense, the doctor replied that it was possible that the illness was contagious and that consequently there was a need to give everyone affected a thorough medical examination immediately. The manager then asked how many residents had already come down with the disease, to which the doctor replied that six residents were ill, but that in his opinion many old people had not come forward for examination. The manager claimed that in his experience of old-age homes, such a number was not significant and that there was, therefore, no necessity to enlist additional medical personnel for the examinations demanded. The doctor went away disgruntled and the subject was closed. In the first case, the manager made use of accepted administrative arguments—lack of a large budget, and in this way underlining the doctor's dependence on Mishan rather than on him, thus avoiding a substantive discussion. In the second instance, in contrast, he pontificated on an essentially medical matter claiming on the basis of his "experience" that no danger of an epidemic was imminent. This is a violation of the doctor's field of expertise and decision making. But the manager was forced to do this since the doctor changed the tone of the argument to include professional considerations—"contagious disease"—and in so doing did not allow the manager to elaborate on and contend his first point in which he acknowledged his responsibility for the supply and quality of the food provisions.

To the control of financial resources and of the staff can be added personal-situational factors that help the manager to sustain his influence. His considerable mobility within the home throughout the day allows direct surveillance of all that transpires within its walls. This mobility is expedited by the unified, high-rise nature of the building, with its multiple, efficient elevator system, by the concentration of public activities and services on the two lower floors, by the intercom loudspeaker system that enables a resident, a staff member, or the manager to be summoned when needed, and finally by the manager happening to live on the premises. The location of the home in an urban area and allowing quick access to the administrative bodies and services associated with it leaves the manager with sufficient time to spend in the place itself, and simultaneously to reinforce his network of outside connections, without relinquishing his internal control.

One of the arguments that the manager uses to justify the system of the homogeneous home is the ability of such an institution to direct its resources and personnel to encourage the elderly to participate in social frameworks. In his opinion, the level of group activity is a measure of his success as a manager and a vindication of his approach toward the care of the aged.[1] As a result of this he encourages the residents to engage in group activity. The overt reason for this is his contention that such activity stimulates the old person, gives them an interest in life, and a sense of well-being and good health. In fact, the creation of the groups owes a great deal to his initiative, and even where independent groups were not set up by him, he succeeded in achieving control and directing their subsequent activities (as will be exemplified in the analysis of the handicrafts group). This raises the question of whether there is not an additional corollary benefit to setting up such planned interest groups, besides its declared contribution to ameliorating the residents' condition. It seems that such circumscribed organization allows the manager to exert even more extensive supervision over residents' activities.

In the home there are fifteen different groups[2] whose activities are encouraged by the manager and that are supported in the form of allocation of venue, the supply of special equipment, and praise for the participants. The more active the group, the more the manager considers it to be deserving of high praise. In the home the following groups are active: language-study classes (at various levels), a "know-your-country" class, a folklore group, a Bible class, a Talmudic study group (operating under the auspices of the synagogue), a handicrafts group, a choir, and exercise, art, and sculpture classes as well as the discussion group. Each group is about fifteen persons strong and the manager claims that this number is too low and points to the anomaly of some residents participating in several groups and others in none at all. The groups mainly convene in the afternoon and the manager makes a point of visiting them almost daily. Some "fringe" groups have been established without a formal green light from the manager, but without raised objections on his part, such as the bridge club. The involvement of the groups with the manager is further cemented by their frequent need to prevail on him to arrange speakers or outside teachers. Often, the participants use this fact to strengthen their ties with him and to demonstrate to him their good functioning by the intensity of their involvement in the group(s). The folklore group, for instance, is organized in such a way as to invite speakers and show films from time to time, a state of affairs requiring the manager's endorsement and cooperation. The members of this circle have tried occasionally to demonstrate their abiding interest in the subject by pressing for an increased level of activities within the group.

The network of group activities allowed the manager to strengthen his direct involvement in the social life of his residents. This involvement was exclusive to him and obviated any dependence on other members of staff in the home since, even when the manager required teachers and lecturers who could be found within the existing staff establishment, he preferred to look outside the precincts. The groups created a wide-ranging potential for the introduction of new subject matter and a forum for the encouragement of individuals in whom the manager was interested. Thus, they served as a channel for the crystallization of social relations according to a pattern determined by the manager. Most of the groups met regularly two or three times a week, mainly in the afternoon. Some groups met almost daily, and in some cases even twice a day.

It is obvious that some of these interest groups were primarily a method for demonstrating how well their members functioned and provided the means whereby the manager could both examine and encourage such functioning. This does not imply that the activities themselves did not possess an interest among the residents or stimulate them to take part, but rather posits that their raison d'être was woven around the system of relations between them and the manager, which essentially conveyed the "message" of proper functioning in its diverse interpretations.

II

The data presented above constitutes part of the framework from which the concept of functioning is derived. The manager asserted repeatedly, in conversation, his ability to determine "objective functioning" impartially for all residents. In practice, reality dictates otherwise and this ability is limited in a number of ways.

51

1) The manager is not the sole arbiter of who is admitted to or removed from the home. In fact, from what I gathered, many would-be residents applied directly to the director of Mishan himself and he personally vouchsafed their acceptance by the home, even becoming involved so far as securing a particular room or floor for them. When one of the residents was asked why he occupied himself with handicrafts in his own room rather than participating in the organized group (which would provide him with a medium par excellence for demonstrating his functioning), he quipped, "That bores me, and besides, the Mishan director is a personal friend—he arranged for my room in the home." His words serve as a form of public announcement, in which the need to demonstrate good functioning is unnecessary for him, since the various aspects involved in the concept are devoid of meaning. Sometimes the resident can boast of a public body as his sponsor or an influential individual with Histadrut connections, which can be exploited to place some applicant in the home. An example of this type is a former activist in one of the South American communities, who in keeping with his role, raised funds for Israel, contributing heavily himself, and participating in Zionist activity in his country. When he arrived in Israel he was admitted to the home by virtue of his connections. He is proud of the fact and in conversation stressed the obligation of the State and its institutions to embrace him.

2) The determination of functioning does not affect the behavior of two other types of resident. First, those aged who declare their intention to leave the home when their powers begin to decline are exempt. Their desire stems principally from an awareness of the inability of the home, under existing conditions, to provide medical or back-up services consonant with their future enfeebled state. Such declarations generally were made by those residents who had better prospects than most to be accepted into a more appropriate institution. For example, a female physician who maintains her contacts with the hospital in which she worked prior to retirement, can, she claims, utilize them to gain admission to a suitable institution for the chronically infirm. The second type of resident is one who, due to the appearance of

physiological and psychological symptoms associated with senescence, is unaware of his surroundings and appears indifferent towards his fate. These residents do not sustain any kind of contact with the others and some of them do little more than to move from their room into the dining room and back again. They have acquired various nicknames from staff and other residents alike, among them "vegetables," "exhibition" (because they spend their time sitting still doing nothing for hours), and "animals" (see chapter 2).

Most other residents respond in one way or another to the challenge of good functioning and I will discuss this in due course. Even when they are in the last stages of their stay in the home—in the sick bay—and the matter of transferring them is all but concluded, many refuse to relinquish their hope to stay on in the home. They effect this by presenting themselves in a manner shaped by their understanding of good functioning. During the manager's sick bay visits some try to present a welcoming face, declaring how well they feel and their certainty of a quick recovery. I recall one women with advanced cancer and aware of it, who despite all her pain presented a smiling exterior during the manager's visit, and claimed she felt a great improvement in her condition. The adjustment of the presentation of self to institutional demands, even in a hopeless situation, attests to the struggle waged by the individual against the fact of their deterioration. Even more than eliciting a favorable response from the manager, there is here a denial of the inevitable, made possible with the aid of the mechanism developed and facilitated by the manager.

The differential quality of the concept of functioning may be seen in the various interpretations attached to it by different residents. Moreover, three dimensions inherent in the concept may be distinguished: *flexibility*—for which there are no clearly adumbrated criteria; *dynamism*—a resident may be considered as functioning well or badly during different periods; and *pressure*— the manager does not expect that the residents will function "according to the book" without his assistance. A resident who has not yet been accredited as functioning well finds herself subjected to the manager's powers of persuasion to modify her behavior. These three dimensions will be made explicit through the exposition of three cases and in so doing it will be possible to take a cursory look at the "moral career" (Goffman 1961c) of three residents in the home.

FLEXIBILITY

One of the manager's most valued residents, Mr. Reuveni,[3] serves as an example of good functioning, although he is blind and ill, finds it hard to get around, and needs the assistance of a guide. Before coming into the home, Mr. Reuveni had been a researcher and had several of his articles published. He is very proud of these publications and claims that he succeeded in contributing to a number of innovations in his chosen field. He was admitted to the home on his own, although he is married, because his wife is considered "bed-ridden," that is, she is unable to take care of herself. Within the home he is very active, heading the Bible study group, preparing lectures, and giving speeches. In his room, he is engaged in a new line of research and utilizes a Braille typewriter, whose acquisition was approved by the manager. In preparing his study group's activities he co-opts the services of one of the leaders of the discussion group—who himself is a member of the "house committee" (the activities of these bodies will be clarified later in chapter 3)—a man close to the manager and holding sway over other residents.

In conversation, Mr. Reuveni stresses his support for the homogeneous character of the home, citing the case of his sick wife to buttress his contention. He claims that their separation has been occasioned by force of circumstance and "Anyhow I couldn't help her and where she is now she gets better medical treatment than she could here." Furthermore, he explains that in principle this form of residential care is preferable to that of the heterogeneous system, since "It is hard to be around the crippled and incapacitated, we cannot help them and they only dampen our spirits." This is yet another indication how the desire to avoid change and halt its progress can, in certain cases, lead to the sacrifice of lifelong emotion-charged ties of considerable weight in the individual's life. This behavior highlights the dilemma of the choice between the perpetuation of emotional ties and their severance in the interests of arresting change.

Mr. Reuveni goes out often, and despite his blindness and illness he takes part in various cultural and social activities in the area. His relations with members of the discussion group are warm, and a number of them visit him in his room. However, Mr. Reuveni does not participate in the meetings of this group, apparently because of their rigidly negative attitude toward the handicapped that occasionally surfaces during these meetings and is liable to rub off on him. His contacts with other residents are limited and ambivalent—on the one hand, during group activities he is listened to attentively, questions are asked, comments made, and appreciation for his lectures expressed. On the other hand, when he stands in front of the dining room waiting with the rest of the residents for the doors to be opened, no one approaches him, and even the same residents who just an hour before were with him in the group now ignore him. Even the person who guided him to where the group was being convened overlooked him completely. It seems that the reason for this lies in Mr. Reuveni's handicap. The attitude in the home toward the incapacitated and crippled is quite complete and will provide the subject matter for detailed analysis in the forthcoming chapters. At this stage, it is sufficient to say that the reservation and avoidance of contact are blatantly characteristic of the attitude of healthy residents toward their more handicapped fellows.

What can be learned from this case about the notion of functioning? Despite his severe physical limitations, this individual was seen as functioning well by the manager, because of his ability to pursue both social and individual activities intensively. This allows the manager to "press home" his contention that the physiological condition of the resident exerts a relatively small impact on his field of activity. Such "proof" is required by the manager, because it helps reinforce his authority as the final arbiter of what constitutes good functioning. If greater weight were given to physical factors, it would tilt the balance of judgment in favor of the physician. Mr. Reuveni helps the manager by providing a "personal example"—the separation from his wife—and by his ideological support for the advantages of the homogeneous institution over its heterogeneous variant. It also explains why the manager sends so many visitors to Mr. Reuveni's room—in order to hear his ideas and become acquainted with the man. Consequently, it can be argued that the relationship between the two does not derive solely from a superior-dependent power equation, but also from what Mr. Reuveni gives the manager in exchange. As a blind man, dependent on others all his life, institutional life does not drastically alter his mode of life, especially since he is given the chance to pursue his research studies, and even to find a "built-in" audience for his lectures.

The other residents do not accept the manager's estimation of Mr. Reuveni's functioning. His noninvolvement in the Discussion Group, and the avoidance behavior directed against him that surfaces in public places, attest to the considerable reservations felt toward him, the sources of which will be clarified later. Of course, he is incapable of looking after himself, requiring help with all his activities and in need of comprehensive medical treatment. But all this notwithstanding, he is defined as "functioning well." We have already indicated the reasons for this, and it is clear that the concept of functioning, despite its formal definition, is subject to flexibility, in that certain constituent factors can be overlooked while others are stressed and still newer ones added. The unusual element in this case is that the fluidity of the label derives not only from Mr. Reuveni's standing outside the home, as is the case of other residents, but principally from the system of relations woven between him and the manager within the institution.

The lack of congruence between the formal definition of Mr. Reuveni's functioning and his standing among the residents hints at the lack of consistency that exists between the latter's fields of control, which build up relations with the manager and the boundaries between the system of cognitive categories of the residents. For the manager, Mr. Reuveni was a threat, since in the eyes of the residents he represents the possibility of deteriorating into a state of nonfunctioning and dependency.

DYNAMICISM

Mrs. Zioni is a widow of Yemenite extraction who was the organizer and initiator of many cultural activities within the home. She organized plays and dances, ran different types of groups, and because of this was considered by the manager to be a resident who made a substantial contribution to the life of the institution. More than once, he extolled her activism and vitality, and presented her as an example of how elderly persons should conduct themselves. Many residents endorsed this view, adding their own words of enthusiastic praise. Some of them claimed that Mrs. Zioni was exceptional in her zest for life and her talent for drawing other elderly people into meaningful activity. Then, quite suddenly, a change occured—Mrs. Zioni stopped participating in the activities of the home, refused to continue running groups, and kept to her room. The manager tried to explain the transformation and to encourage her to resume her activities. In this he failed, and after his efforts came to naught, he concluded sadly that Mrs. Zioni was an example of an old person who had regressed from a state of good functioning to that of poor functioning. He classed her with the vegetables—those old people who do nothing, and, from his pronouncements on the subject, it seemed her days in the home were numbered. However, within a short period of time, Mrs. Zioni resumed her activities again, thus returning to the fold of the "good functioners." The other residents saw this as proof of the possibility of combating the imposition of a social label through sheer willpower.

Mrs. Zioni constructed the definition of her functioning through her own actions within the home, for she was not one of those residents with powerful outside connections. When these earlier behaviors changed or ceased altogether—behaviors that the manager defined as positive—the evaluation of the effectiveness of her functioning changed with it. In this case, in contrast to the case cited earlier, there was full agreement between the manager and the residents in their conceptions of what had happened.

Pressure

A third dimension of the concept of functioning is that of the operation of *pressure*. The manager habitually lectures the residents about the importance of activity in the home for the creation of a feeling of well being and health. But over and above this, he approaches certain residents in whom he is most interested. Mrs. Tzifroni, a widow, was a renowned private physician with a large number of patients. She was heavily involved in public affairs, especially in the professional association to which she belonged. A few years previously her health had failed, and she was forced to retire. She claimed that she had never contemplated living in an old-age home but "was dragged in by friends." In her view, the home is "a boardinghouse designed for rest, and no more." She spends most of the morning in town where she busies herself with family matters ("I have a large family") and with meeting friends. She still receives invitations to medical conventions and courses, and takes great

57

pride in this fact. Some of her former patients continue to visit her in the home, and even seek professional advice. In the home itself, she has volunteered to help out in the sick bay, but is reluctant to go beyond this. Any spare time is devoted to reading and to gatherings of the friends she has acquired in the home, whom she calls "the Russian intelligentsia" (apparently to distinguish them from members of the discussion group who are considered by the residents to be the "intelligentsia" of the home). These get-togethers take place in the residents' rooms and are not encouraged by the management. The manager has sought to persuade Mrs. Tzifroni to broaden her activities on behalf of the home, to show more interest in the various groups and in the lectures accompanying them, to write for the local paper, and to strike a chord with those residents with whom he personally is close (mainly the members of the discussion group). Mrs. Tzifroni will not countenance this. While she praises the manager as being "an excellent administrator" and for "his individual relationship with the elderly," she is still not interested in participating in groups organized by him, or in taking advantage of "the goodies thrown at us by the Histadrut." Despite her refusal, the manager is still at pains to integrate her into the formal social framework of the home, and persists in his efforts to convince her. The other residents see in Mrs. Tzifroni a striking example of resistance to change, and of self-control. Thus, to a great extent their view contradicts the manager's claim of exclusivity for the institutionalization of functioning, as he defines it.

The pressure exerted by the manager on Mrs. Tzifroni is intensive, but ultimately unproductive. Why? There are several reasons. Mrs. Tzifroni is not compelled to reside in the home, for she can embrace a wide number of residential alternatives outside the institution (being well-to-do), and therefore does not feel constrained to demonstrate good functioning at any price. She does not see herself as belonging to the home, and takes pains to emphasize her close ties with the outside world, her activities outside the institution, and her circle of friends within it, whose relations are based on personal factors, devoid of any institutional constraint. Her view of the home as a place designed for rest and the provision of basic amenities, but with pointless social activities, makes her a resident who has not accepted an institutional framework intended to cater exclusively to her needs. According to her conception, the home is intended to satisfy only some of her basic needs and thus does not constitute a total institution. The manager's attempts at persuasion are directed in fact to effect a change in this perception and to transform the home into an all-embracing framework for her. The alternatives open to her, her useful contacts outside the home, and her view of the home, create for her a situation of minimum totality.

The manager's inability to convince residents like Mrs. Tzifroni to take on roles in the home and thus join the ranks of the good functioners is not seen by him to be a personal failure, nor as a result of the alternatives open to these individuals outside or because of any inadequacies within the home itself. He believes that as people get older, their desire for social activity and contact with others lessens. He claims that this is an inevitable and unstoppable process. Consequently, blame should not be cast on the old person's environment, but rather on the individual themself. (In the case of Mrs. Tzifroni this argument is patently invalid, since despite her loose ties with the organized frameworks within the home, she maintains close bonds with the outside world, and with other residents.) Since the manager is interested in the professional literature on old age, especially its psychosociological aspects, he is attracted to the disengagement theory of Cumming and Henry (*Growing Old*, 1961), which supports his own stand regarding the inevitable dissociation of old people from society.

The instance of Mrs. Tzifroni serves to extend our understanding of a number of other aspects of the home. The manager's ability to invade the private lives of his residents is contingent also on the latter's wishes, no less than on the force of his own personality. While not every resident can withstand such pressures, nonetheless the character of the living conditions within the home is clearly the result of mutual contacts between the residents and the manager, with the latter influenced by the wishes and actions of the former. Until now we have seen that these reciprocal relations generally do not break down into open conflict. Many other cases support the assumption that the residents and the manager usually reach a *modus vivendi* concerning their mutual expectations of each other. Nevertheless, open conflicts do arise, and will be described in due course. In the continuous "negotiation" waged between the manager and the residents, the manager exploits his formal authority in order to realize his aims. However, he often exercises this power not by enforcing his wishes, but rather through the expedient of restraint. Two examples will help to illustrate the point:

In the previous chapter, it was noted that residents are not allowed to bring private articles into their rooms. Yet the enforcement of this regulation is complicated and entails endless arguments with the residents involved. The manager himself admits that old people are sometimes deeply attached to artifacts from their former homes. On the other hand, permission to retain a prized article can be used by the manager as a spur to elicit cooperation from a resident in whom he is interested. For example, permission granted to a resident to keep a sewing machine in her room was reciprocated by her participation in the home's activities.

Another example: according to regulations, a resident is not entitled to be employed outside the home. Enforcement of this rule is also fraught with difficulties (since the home is not closed and there are many part-time and temporary jobs open to residents). In certain cases, the manager turns a blind eye even though the resident knows that he is aware of the fact. Moreover, he understands the manager's reluctance to act against him—for as long as cooperation exists between them, his outside employment will not be endangered,[4] and the manager's need for a naked display of power will be unnecessary.

Another method, albeit a very rare one, which fosters cooperation, comes into play when the manager allows a resident to enter his private quarters to engage in personal relations over and above the accepted role relations in the home. The manager, although being resident, differentiates sharply between his family life and his work. Management of the home is carried out exclusively from his office, and his flat is closed to residents. One case I know of attests to the possibility of resident penetration into the manager's private quarters and, as a result, close cooperation between them. One of the residents, a woman enjoying strong ties with her family outside the home, as well as high social status, requested to join the handicrafts group. There ensued a sharp difference of opinion between the residents and other members of the group resulting in her being forced to leave the group. The woman went straight to the manager's flat and tearfully informed him of her expulsion from the group, even requesting his intervention. The manager, for whom good relations with the group were of the utmost importance, calmed her and persuaded her to forego her involvement in it and to occupy herself by decorating the home is another way. As a result of this conversation and the personal relations that developed in its wake, the resident's family donated a very valuable work of art to the home.

60

The sociological measurement of the concept of functioning depends on the different types of relationships prevailing between the manager and the residents in the home. These relations depend on the residents' ties with the outside world, or their activity within the home, and on the way they view the institution as providing a full or only partial backdrop to their lives. These characteristics vary, not only for each resident, but sometimes over a period of time for the same resident. Since the definition of a resident's functioning provides one of the prime sources of power for the manager, and as a result of this, a principal motivation for resident activity, the sociological significance of this concept is central to the understanding of the organization of life in the institution. Thus, we find that it is a tool in the war against change, which serves the interests of both the manager and the residents. This tool is characterized by its flexibility and by its considerable dynamism in negotiating relationships and in differentiating amongst the residents.

The complexities and varieties of functioning can serve as a yardstick for examining the nature of the relation between authority and power vested in a formal organization, represented by a manager, and the behavior patterns of the residents against the background of their social and cultural environment.

III

The juxtaposition of the outside world with the framework of the total institution has interested a number of researchers. Goffman (1961a, 120) speaks about the differing degrees of impermeability of the total institution to the reality external to it. Etzioni (1964, 71) classifies types of organizations according to the extent to which they can be permeated by outside norms or by their attempt to create their own norms, the latter type incorporating total institutions. This view is endorsed by Giallombardo (1966, 287–88) who endeavors to understand the connection between the cultural system outside the prison she studied, and the normative framework created within it. Until now the focus of interest and of diagnosis has been normative—behavioral. However, it should also be asked what is the nature of the relations between the home and its surroundings from the standpoint of the possibility of pouring resources into it and of activating forces emanating from the outside? Rosengren and Lefton (1969, 101) claim that the greater the connection of the institution to the governing elite of the community in which it exists, the greater the choices of extending better services to the residents (inmates). This generalization fails to distinguish between the ability of different residents themselves to mobilize resources and various power sources. As we have seen in the earlier descriptions, this facility is not uniform, and old people enjoy different potentials to enlist outside corrections in order to influence their standing within the home. It appears, therefore, that the home is unable to direct every resident's behavior to an equal degree, and that this is not only because of the institutional underlife.

The outside connections intended to enlist power and resources do not exhaust all the relationships of the residents with the society outside the institution. Many residents, whether or not they enjoy these external power sources, regard individuals singly or in groups outside the home as sources of identification, or of aloofness, or, at any rate, a focus for positive or negative comparative reference.[5] Consequently, one should distinguish between the resident's social network outside the home, which he can manipulate as a source of power, and his relationship to different groups outside the institution, with members with which he has no social connections.

Clearly a resident's ties with the outside world change the pattern of his or her relationships with other residents and with the staff. In this section we will deal with the latter—What precisely is the nature of the old person's relationships with the staff? In the literature a number of approaches to treatment of this problem can be found. Most prominent is the view of Goffman (1961a), who claims that the staff do not see the residents as human beings at all, but as so much material to be "molded" and adapted to the institution (1961a, 16). As a result of this, the process of mortification of self is one through which all residents must pass. Since we have here a reified conception of the character of the resident, an unbridgeable gap exists between staff and residents (1961a, 6), although it is feasible to distinguish different degrees of severity (1961a, 118) depending on the institution concerned. Other researchers (Belknap 1956, Dunham and Weinberg 1960) agree with Goffman that the attitude shown to inmates in a considerable number of total institutions is appalling, but in their opinion this does not arise from the staff view of residents as inferior. Rather, it is the chronic shortage of resources, administrative obstacles, and the limited number of staff who are needed to deal with a large number of inmates that causes such an attitude to develop. Support for this viewpoint is offered by Rosengren and Lefton (1969, 85–86), who point out that in total institutions in which the inmates enjoy high social status and considerable means, the staff do not regard them as inferior, and often feel themselves to be on a lower social level than their charges. The researchers think this arises from the status enjoyed by the inmates outside the institution.[6]

In the old-age home under discussion, both ways of looking at the residents prevail. Professional members of staff see certain residents as more respectable and important than they themselves. This is mainly because of their prior status and present contacts outside the home, whereas other residents were seen by them as "vegetables," "still-life," or simply "not functioning," and these are usually candidates for transfer, lacking as they do outside contacts. Until now a parallel has been drawn between the staff view of the resident and their outside connections, yet cases do exist where the resident is defined as a vegetable but is not removed, precisely because of these ties. In private conversations amongst the staff, tension occasionally arises because of the institutional definition of the resident as a vegetable—that is, suitable for removal—and the practical inability to effect this. Concerning the nonprofessional staff, no importance is attached to the resident's outside ties (for a resident is unable to bring about the dismissal of a junior member of the staff except in exceptional circumstances) and, therefore, a gap exists between their view of the residents as a whole, as useless old people, and their daily contacts with them that sometimes involve the giving of gifts and the provision of better services to one resident or another. Overall it can be said that a different view does exist in regard to different residents and that this view is generally parallel to the residents' standing and connection outside the home. However, this connection, as has been noted, is equivocal.

The ties of the residents with the outside, the amount of time spent outside the home, relations with the staff, and the latter's ability to influence and control them are all different aspects of the totality prevailing within the institution. Since these aspects vary by their very nature and force from resident to resident, it is possible to speak of degrees of totality within the same institution, rather than of an "underlife" (Goffman 1961b).

Wallace (1971, 3) suggests examining different institutions according to their degree of totality. Sykes (1966, 45) notes that even in a well-guarded prison, the ability of staff to exercise power over prisoners and thus to influence their behavior is restricted. Bennett (1963) tried to evolve indices in order to distinguish varying degrees of totality in different old-age homes, primarily according to their respective regulations—what is customarily allowed or forbidden in each. Perhaps such differentiations between institutions, relative to the degree of totality would be more accurate and fruitful if it were possible to specify different types and levels of totality within the same institution, with respect to different residents. Some old people enjoy the option of living outside the home, and this is reflected in their attitude toward it and the organization of their life within it. Some spend a good part of their time outside the home, and in so doing extricate themselves from the definition of the total institution, where all aspects of their lives are under the control of a single authority (Goffman 1961a, 6), a central characteristic of such an institution. Moreover, certain residents effectively participate in the running of the home, and in determining modes of conduct and evaluation within it, thus transforming themselves into part of the authority system in the eyes of other residents. These differences between residents validate the attempt to differentiate among different types of totality within the same institution.

So far we have dealt principally with the relations between the staff and residents against the background of the differing power bases of different residents. A second system of relations that shapes the organization of life in the home consists of the ties and the evaluations existing among the residents themselves. One of the factors creating such partial totality is the existence of these ties, as in the case when a resident acquires a position of strength within the home, and gains advantages over the other residents.[7] However, the crucial area of these relations with which we will deal are the distinctions drawn by the old people among themselves, according to various criteria. It has already been noted that individuals with a specific background characterized by special traits and symbols (dress, speech, area of interest) are considered to be the home's "elite." Other residents associated with a different set of characteristics (aimless sitting around, faulty speech, slovenly dress) are classified as "vegetables," "exhibition," "animals," and so on, and are given the lowest status amongst the old people.

This distinction between various classes of old people raises a question that is appropriate to pose at this stage—What is the meaning of old age in an old-age home, that is, in a concentration of old people? Kastenbaum and Durkee (1964a, 1964b) indicate that in a sample they collected in an old-age home in which the average age was eighty, only half of those sampled defined themselves as aged, the others not accepting such a label. It appears that in the home studied all the residents recognize their old age,[8] but the real difficulty is in deciding what kind of old person the resident is, in relation to their fellows.

In essence, this is a question of definition of identity that is imposed in part by the power structure in the home; that is, the division into different categories of residents is partly a result of the management's policy and the bureaucratic forces within which that policy operates. At the same time, this component is definitely not the only dimension that fashions the resident's identity. This identity is entangled in a world of contradictory and unclear cognitive categories interwoven with specific areas of control and sources of power. It is a fluid and unstructured reality, which prevents setting up clear and unequivocal standards for defining situations and attitudes.

In the next three chapters, we will see how, in the framework of the dynamics of social relations current in three groups of residents, a clearer identity of the participants emerges. We will trace the mechanisms that shape the relations between the disunified worlds of meaning, and the various power complexes in the home. Moreover, we will try to suggest the guiding principle informing these relations and claim that in all cases it entails the prevention of change, an act assuming different nuances, according to the circumstances and bonds prevailing in the groups and their constituent members.

It should be emphasized that the choice of three groups is incidental, and certainly does not represent the entire spectrum of reactions and situations existing in the home. All the groups are formal, in the sense that they operate with the knowledge and approval of the management, but this should not be taken to mean that the informal organization, which was not studied, is unimportant.

4. The Discussion Group

This group is considered by its own participants, the manager, and other residents alike to constitute the home's "elite," and this designation is widely accepted in references to its members. The way this situation has evolved will be clarified forthwith, but at this stage a number of questions will be posed that will serve as an introduction to the presentation of material relating to the group: How do the workings of the group bear on the life-style of its members as a reference group for residents who are not participants? Is it feasible that this group will pressure other residents into accepting the authority of the institution? These questions can be examined from several analytical standpoints: the group's relations with the manager,[1] the sources of its power, and the struggles for influence between the two, and its relations with other residents. How do its members view themselves as compared with other old people in the home, and emerging from this is the central question that will occupy us: How do the group members organize their own world of meaning?

I

At the beginning of 1972 the discussion group was born. Its ascribed function was to debate different topics raised by its members. Toward this end, it began convening meetings regularly to which some thirty residents were invited.

The initiative for the establishment of the group came from one of the residents, Mr. Amit, who had been a high-ranking army officer, held several public offices, and had been involved both in his army and civilian career with matters of jurisdiction and inspection. Staff and residents both held him in openly expressed esteem, and his name was spoken with great reverence. His residence in the home signified that, in the eyes of the resident population, the home was an estimable place, since he had actually opted to live there when, befitting his status, he could have chosen any other place of retirement. Mr. Amit proposed the group meet every week, the members be selected by personal invitation only, and that different problems should be debated in the course of the sessions. The manager acceded and began issuing invitations to those residents whom Mr. Amit wished to invite. These were people with some sort of experience of public life, teachers, members of free professions, and others thought suitable by Mr. Amit. Some of them were very well known outside the home and a few had become almost "national symbols." To illustrate this, a newspaper article relating to two of the members is presented. (The journalist responsible is not generally given to hyperbole).[2]

They are the eternal pioneers, the pavers of roads, the triumphant innovators of Jewish labor, amongst the first volunteers for the Jewish Brigade[3] and the Haganah,[4] the audacious conquerors of the wilderness,[5] in the vanguard of immigration. Just call them and they will come. Give them a goal and a challenge and they are behind you. They are two of a race of titans.[6] Amongst those appearing on the landscape, always marching at the fore with quiet dignity, steadfastly and modestly. Possessions? Money?—never interested them.

A cursory linguistic analysis of the symbolic code inherent in the contents of this quotation reveals the absence of a chronological time scale (use of the present tense, although the events described occurred in the past), and the use of expressions drawn from the national myth (audacious, titans) of a grandiose and exclusive nature. We have here a detailed expression of the national myth resistant to the transformation wrought by changing times and reality.

The first meeting was devoted to the topic "The Attitude of the U.S.S.R. Towards the Jews." Following the proceedings, the group's secretary, Mr. Nachmani, wrote letters to the Mishan directorate, to the Labor Party journal, to the Foreign Ministry, and to the secretary-general of the United Nations in which the group branded the words of the USSR.'s UN representative on his country's attitude towards the Jews as a pack of lies. The next meeting dealt with the subject of "Retirement Problems," and subsequent to this the group's activities were interrupted due to the illness of its chairman, Mr. Amit.

Before giving a general description of the group's activity and a detailed analysis of two events connected with this activity, I will attempt to present a picture of the nature of the group's membership, by citing as an example the life history of one member prior to her admission to the home and inclusion in the group.

Mrs. Shoshani was a teacher who arrived in Israel in the early twenties ("I was a pioneer"), taught in various schools of the "Labor stream"[7] and was active in public affairs—she claims children's education was her chief goal in life, and in pursuing it she neglected her family and her private interests. In her opinion, education today does not achieve its aims, and children do not "absorb values" or see their teachers as "personal examples." She is very proud of her pupils, noting that some of them today enjoy high positions in the government, the army, and the educational system. A few of them even visit her in the home. She retired only when forced to through illness, as she literally collapsed in the classroom while teaching— with this dramatic end of her teaching career being retold by her on different occasions. When she came into the home, she wanted only to "take life easy." But the manager began to persuade her to participate in activities, and even designated her the editor of the house. For some months she refused his entreaties, but finally consented to assume the editorial chair. Moreover, Mrs. Shoshani began to participate in the celebration and observance of festivals, to recite some of her writings publicly, and to organize cultural activities. She quickly gained the esteem of the other residents, and ultimately was invited to participate in the discussion group where her contribution was judged to be worthy of attention and admiration.

Mrs. Shoshani is meticulous about precise and polished Hebrew usage and attributes her success amongst the residents to this fact. There appears to be some justification in her assertion, for several residents alluded to her command of Hebrew when talking about her. Her attitude toward the younger generation is surprisingly ambivalent. On the one hand, she argues no effort should be spared in granting young people attention and resources and she is proud of her ties with them. Nevertheless, she is critical of the heartless attitude of the young towards the elderly, their intolerance and their unconcealed scorn. She blames a defective educational system for this situation, and especially "the shocking error perpetrated in the country when the Labor stream was abolished." Her attitude toward the crippled is wary—she feels that they should be helped to the utmost, but that at the same time they should be transferred to another institution.

Several characteristics of Mrs. Shoshani are also applicable to most of the other members of the discussion group: significantly, all had an active life prior to their admission to the home; the absence of a time lapse between their retirement and admission; an emphasis on educational interests and public affairs; strong ties with the outside world; stress on "pioneering" and "national" values; fastidiousness in the correct use of Hebrew; performance of several different functions within the home; ambivalence toward the younger generation; and reservations about the existence of the handicapped in the home. These points will be explicated in the description of the following events.

Mrs. Shoshani herself had not fulfilled any central public role as had some of the members of the discussion group. Among them were several who by virtue of their personalities and actions had become, as previously pointed out, "national symbols" esteemed by most of the public, while others are interviewed for the newspapers periodically, or take part in radio programs. For most of them, their present residence in the home is hard to accept, and they offer various rationalizations for this state of affairs. At any rate, all of them could have exploited reasonable residential alternatives outside the home, something that largely determines their attitude towards the place (as will be shown in due course).

The social networks of members of the discussion group outside the group are extremely varied. Some conduct most aspects of their social life outside the home, often with well-known public figures. Others have developed close ties with several group members, although this is not connected with their group membership. The only group of which it can be said that relationships derived directly from participation in the group itself is the body calling itself the "house committee," comprising Mr. Amit and two other founding members. They claim that they were elected by the group to fulfill this function, but many residents have no recollection of this. They maintain close contact with the manager, and the topics to be discussed by the group are raised by them. In the absence of the chairman, one of the members of the house committee conducts the meeting. The house committee even has ties with the director of Mishan, and according to Mr. Amit, was charged with the responsibility for employment in the home. (The significance of this will be discussed

70

in the chapter on the handicrafts group.) The manager does not overreact to this declaration because an identity of interests exists between him and the director of Mishan in regard to employment in the home; the house committee can assist him in the recruitment of many residents for work in the handicrafts group. In spite of the lack of a reaction by the manager, it is possible to see in this the germ of a later development with the attempt to establish a disciplinary court. It appears that the house committee began its attempts to exert control over the life of the institution in the area of employment, but that this attempt did not lead to a confrontation between it and the manager.

The manager participates in group meetings, but has to request the floor from Mr. Amit. He is not allowed to interrupt the other speakers, and his contributions must be kept within the time allocation. The discussions are conducted with proper seriousness and in an orderly manner. Those wishing to speak inform the chairman and await their turn. Heckling is absolutely forbidden, with speakers taking care to stick to the point, and to use the clearest and most understandable language possible—permission must be sought to speak in any language other than Hebrew. For example, when in one meeting a female participant weighed in with a spat of heckling, Mr. Amit upbraided her with the reprimand: "Mrs. Paz, you come from the executive committee (of the Histadrut) and know how a meeting is conducted. Why are you interrupting?" This provides evidence that the rules of behavior and their implementation pertaining to the group do not derive from the reality of the home, but are adopted, apparently in a completely conscious way, from patterns of activity "implanted" by group members from their experiences outside the home.

II

A brief description of a chain of events demonstrates the role of the manager in the group. One day a man, who introduced himself as a representative of Magen David Adom, entered the conference room (the home's clubroom) in order to sell raffle tickets.

He requested the help of the management towards this end. The manager asked him to come to his office after the meeting in order to sort out the matter. Mr. Amit objected to this, saying that it was only right for the man to be referred to the residents and their representatives, since it was to them that he intended to sell the tickets. The man stayed on to explain his purpose in coming to the home. The manager did not react to Mr. Amit's words. This incident, too, can be viewed as an attempt to take part in the running of the home, on this occasion the purpose being to determine relations with the outside world. Many participants felt that the home should cease being a "hothouse" and should develop relations with the outside. Apparently, this issue was not seen as crucial enough to merit a spirited reply.

Various residents proposed establishing a group for visiting the elderly sick that would involve home visits to solitary individuals. Toward this end a budget was required for travelling expenses and for gifts, but the manager refused to authorize this. Yet, when at a discussion group meeting, one of the participants proposed establishing the aforementioned circle, the manager immediately stated he regarded this initiative as "a humane and noble activity," and even offered his help in granting funds to the group once it was established. This incident illustrates the transformation of the group into a power base for residents, who are able to achieve results that they could not otherwise attain. The reason for this is rooted, as was noted, in the importance the manager attaches to the continued operation of the group as a means of attaining reinforcement and support for his principal policy lines in regard to the nature of the home. The undermining of these positions could limit the areas of his influence—with the professional staff, etc. Likewise, the manager is afraid of quarreling with the leaders of the group because of their status within the home, but even more so because of their standing outside it. In the incident described, the proposal was raised by the editor of the newspaper and seconded by Mr. Amit, two individuals with considerable influence with the home, the editor internally and Mr. Amit by virtue of his links outside the home. The manager is interested in cooperating with them, even if this involves minor concessions.

The final case occurred at a meeting in which a woman member demanded the restrictions on residents being gainfully employed be revoked. She stated that she keeps a sewing machine in her room (which was against the rules), and moreover, that she sometimes lends it to a lady friend so that she can use it profitably. She appealed to other residents to learn from her example and follow her lead. The manager did not react, but hurriedly changed the subject. It is possible that if this subject had been raised elsewhere the manager would have tried to persuade the resident, or even to demand, that she cease this illicit activity. In this context, however, he did not do so, since it would have invited a clash with the whole group. Such a confrontation, as we shall see later, is a definite possibility with uncertain results.

Why is the manager interested in the continued existence of the group? How does this activity function as a reaction to the situation of the group's members as residents of an old-age home? With the help of the following case, it will be possible to consider these problems.

III

Following a meeting whose topic matter was "Retirement on the Kibbutz" (inspired by a series of articles appearing at the time in the newspaper *Ha'aretz*), it was decided to continue debating the problems of the aged and a meeting was convened to discuss "old age institutions." The debate was chaired by a substitute chairman— since Mr. Amit was still hospitalized—who gave the manager the floor. The latter described the problem of the shortage of beds for the elderly and the tremendous pressure exerted by applicants wishing to be accepted by the home ("fifteen candidates for each bed, two thousand accepted and awaiting admission"). He proposed subdividing the subject into five areas:

1) What is the motivation prompting an application for admission?
2) Can highly developed community services provide a viable alternative to the old-age home?
3) Which kind of institution is preferable—"heterogeneous" or "homogeneous"?
4) Should institutions be built near cities?
5) Should retirement be effected over time or in "one fell swoop"?

Except for the first question, all these are issues designed to raise problems that disturb the manager, although he has answers

73

for them, which he expects will be supported by the discussion group members. An affirmative reply to the second question negates the rationale of the home's existence.[8] Opting for the heterogeneous alternative in point three would undermine the basis of the manager's style and endanger his very position as manager. A negative response to the fourth question casts doubt on the adaptability of the institution to its surroundings, whereas a position on the fifth question that justifies fixed retirement would vitiate the stand of the manager for graduated retirement, and his program for its implementation. Responses supporting the manager's position are important to him, not only because they facilitate the smooth running of the home by eliciting the support of the discussion group and their powerful influence over other residents. In addition, and even more importantly, because of the ties of the group members with the Histadrut institutions (including Mishan), they have the potential of influencing Mishan's policy in the planning of its institutions and the allocation of resources for their establishment and development.

After his presentation of these questions, a dead silence prevailed, not on account of a reluctance to participate, but rather, as later became evident, in order to prepare and formulate what was to be said. The chairman emphasized in his opening remarks that those wishing to speak should indicate their desire, await their turn, and speak concisely, clearly, and to the point, and this indeed was what happened. The chairman noted the contributions and determined the order of participation, so that every speaker rose and reacted to the questions in a set pattern. Any deviation from the subject, over-elaboration, repetition of previous points, or lack of fluency was greeted harshly by the chairman and others present.[9]

In response to the first question, references were made mainly to the following factors for entering the home: social, physical, and emotional isolation, or as some speakers put it: "the feeling of being the fifth wheel." Some felt this feeling sprang from cognizance of the financial independence of their children, thus ensuring "no further need of us." Many mentioned the attitudes of the young as one of the key reasons for their admission to the home. This contention was supported by many participants, who cited the scorn and disdain accorded to them by children. At the same time, they themselves took pains to emphasize that they related to children and young people very positively, and that they were only too happy to see them progress and develop.

74

When consideration of this topic had been exhausted, one of the group leaders, a man holding several important functions in the home (organizer of the Hebrew study groups, on the editorial committee of the house newspaper, and suchlike), described, in a voice choked with emotion, an incident that had happened to him some days before the meeting. While walking in the street, he was deliberately tripped by a youth of about fourteen. He stumbled and fell and the boy laughed at him. When he got up he asked the youth why he had done it, to which the boy allegedly answered: "Because you're old." To this the man replied: "Do you know who an old person is? An old person is someone who did not die young." These words were greeted with silence in the room. Several women sighed deeply and other stories of a similar nature began to circulate, although the incidents depicted were less shocking. The manager, who wanted to bring the discussion back to the original subject, noted that the subject was too important to debate without sufficient preparation, and suggested holding a special debate on the topic. At the suggestion of one participant it was decided to convene a meeting on the subject of "Old Age—Season of Harvest or Casting Off?"

When the participants were asked to consider the question of community services, negative and critical opinions were expressed about this or that service being "a joke," "a game," "not serious," "not solving life's problem." Some related their experience in day centers, even going so far as to claim that the institutional framework is the only solution to the problems of loneliness and alienation from which the old person suffers.

After this approving support for the institutional framework, the debate on the question of the more desirable form of institution, homogeneous or heterogeneous, got under way. The manager invited those present to openly express their opinions and not to hesitate to criticize. However, before giving the members of the group the floor, the manager announced Mishan was about to establish a large institution for the chronically sick, thus forestalling any possible complaints about the lack of suitable facilities in Mishan. He added that his goal was to provide the residents with services, over and above food and lodging, "like in the old-fashioned almshouse" (the manager meant this pejoratively),[10] in fact, to transform the home into a center of social activity for those resident there.

At first there were mixed reactions. One of the participants proposed the criteria for accepting residents should not be altered, but that those residents who became ill should be allowed to remain in the home. The manager responded that such a proposal was unfair, since there should be no double standard surrounding criteria for entering or leaving the home and that the homogeneous character of the home should be vouchsafed. The reactions of most of those present were considerably stronger than even those of the manager. Some charged that any resident whose state of health had seriously deteriorated should be immediately removed, without regard to his or her personal feelings. Two supporting arguments were offered: the extra burden on the staff, and the resulting depression that would "infect" the healthier residents. In support of their contention, several participants cited examples of residents who had been removed. One of these examples, adumbrated at greater length than the other, concerned a woman who fractured her leg and was removed, notwithstanding her objections and her efforts to demonstrate good functioning. Those individuals stressed she was receiving devoted care at the institution to which she had been removed and that the manager had done the right thing in making her leave. Another example was one of the woman physician enjoying close ties with medical institutions, who declared that she had demanded her own removal should she become ill, even if she herself should object in the event. This woman, like many others in the group, has many alternatives open to her for care outside the home, and her words should be seen against this background.

During the proceedings, other speakers mentioned the subject of death. But immediately after doing so excused themselves with such words as: "nonsense," "a joke," "not appropriate to talk about it," etc. It seems there is a barrier the residents impose between themselves and the handicapped and the final phase of death. The existence of this barrier became even clearer in the strong opposition to the proposal of one resident to establish an institution incorporating a number of departments for different types of old people. The others silenced her with noisy heckling (a very rare occurrence within the group), and yet others branded this proposal whose significance involved progressive deterioration until death as "terrible." At the end of the debate on this topic, all the participants agreed that the present framework should be maintained, and that even more stringent rules for entry and removal should be invoked, the sole yardstick being the physical situation of the resident, and not his social integration or mental state.

The last two questions (big city or country, gradual retirement) did not get much of an airing and general agreement was voiced with the manager's position concerning them.

How can the devoted adherence of the leaders of the group to a homogeneous institution be explained? The residents participating in the group, almost to a person, enjoy many residential alternatives to their being in the home. They did not experience any difficulty in gaining admission, and the matter of formal functioning does not serve as a yardstick for evaluation in their cases. Thus, their doubts about being in the institution, and their rationalizations for being there, are greater than for other residents who had no other choices. The spirited support of the homogeneous institution in its existing form derives not only from their desire to support the manager's stand (as has been seen and will be evidenced even more strikingly in due course, the group is not always unqualified in its support). A process of rationalization, designed to justify their choice of the home and to remove any vestige of doubt concerning the correctness of their course of action also plays a significant part. The group support and the pressure exerted on dissident elements reinforced their opinions, and lessened the gap that perhaps existed between other options and the choice that was in fact made.[11,12]

How is this episode to be analyzed? The management of the meeting, the manner of speech employed and its contents—all refer to the social reality outside the institution. In that reality, stress is laid on ambivalent relations with the young whom they admire, but who at the same time evoke fear because of their tendency to deride and scorn the aged. The group's attitude towards other elderly residents is shaped by the latter's physical state and an unequivocal demand to remove the handicapped and seriously ill from the home. It seems that their attitude to themselves is also governed by the yardstick of their health (witness the incident with the old man and the youth and their own insistence on removal in case of illness, etc.). It is true that support for the manager was evident, but was this a result of a desire to reinforce his views, or does perhaps the "rationalization" explanation appear more likely? How do the various characteristics described combine in determining the relations of the group members with other residents and with the manager? What is the source of the insistence on a physiological criterion? This group generally deals with intellectual pursuits. It would be reasonable to expect that its members would use cognitive criteria

77

for their own self-evaluation and the evaluation of others. We will attempt to answer these questions following an analysis of the affair of the disciplinary court.

IV

Various residents in the home—either as a result of their functioning status as old people, or intentionally from spite—engage in actions that disturb other residents and hinder the smooth running of the home. These include giving bribes to domestic staff who clean the rooms, making off with food from the dining room or kitchen and causing spillage on the way to their rooms, holding elevator doors open for long periods, throwing away rubbish in the corridors and not in the special bins provided for this purpose, leaving the toilets and bathtubs soiled after use, playing radios and T.V.s at full volume, violent pushing, appearing slovenly dressed, knocking over cigarette butt receptacles on the carpets, and so on. With the addition of several more items, this list was drawn up by the house committee as examples of acts that must be eliminated, and the matter was brought to the manager for discussion.

The manager agreed that such behaviors constituted a difficult problem, but claimed that he was trying to deal with them quietly—inviting residents for a explanatory session in which the perpetrators were given to understand indirectly why their behavior was offensive and how they should behave in the home. The manager admitted that he did not attach much value to these conversations, since the offenders soon reverted to their offensive behavior; he explained this recidivism in terms of the special social background of some of the deviants, by their former life-styles, and by the diseases of old age—that is, by factors that cannot be altered.

The house committee proposed that the matter be referred to the discussion group. There, Mr. Amit argued that the solution to the problem lay in imposing the jurisdiction of a disciplinary court on the residents concerned, to be administered by the house committee that should have the authority to warn, to reprimand publicly, and in extreme cases to use other measures such as a recommendation to expel the offender from the home. The manager opposed this proposal, claiming that he knew from experience that the establishment of such a court would prove ineffective, because the root causes

78

of the troublesome behavior were not subject to change. According to him, the residents concerned would not be deterred, while at the same time an atmosphere of suspicion, spite, and threats would be created in the home. Mr. Amit still insisted that the subject should be raised at the next group meeting, and that if accepted, the court should indeed be established. The manager could not oppose this step, because in doing so he might endanger the very existence of the group and injure the sensitivities of its leaders. In such a case, his relations with factions outside the home would also be placed at risk.

Preparations for the decisive meeting were extensive both on the part of the manager and that of the house committee. The manager admitted to me at this time that he did not believe anything could prevent the adoption of a resolution supporting the establishment of the court, because,

> Mr. Amit is a charismatic figure and the residents are in awe of him and will follow him blindly. You know what Mr. Amit's standing is in the home? He is trying to introduce military discipline in the place. I understand his line of thought, but I do not think that such methods will be successful.

Actually, the manager was apprehensive about the setting up of the court, in contrast to his position on the matter of part-time employment, because of the likelihood of disharmony and contradiction arising between his interests and those of the house committee. One of the main sources of the manager's power is his determination of the residents' functioning. The creation of a court could jeopardize this power base, since a body comprising residents could intervene and decide which residents were fulfilling expectations, and determine how to react to deviant behavior. The residents might then behave according to the standards laid down by the court, and management of institutional life might be thus wrested from the manager; moreover, a stage might someday, be reached in which the court would demand to exercise jurisdiction in the area of admission to and removals from the home with the backing of the heads of Mishan, with the manager unable to oppose such moves. Such hints could be detected in Mr. Amit's remarks about the court's intention to threaten with expulsion those recalcitrants who would not obey its rulings. Another indication of his thinking came to light in a

79

meeting of the group in which Mr. Amit criticized the Mishan management for accepting "invalids and incapacitated individuals incapable of taking care of themselves, who created a burden and an annoyance to the healthier population of residents." In his opinion, this was a serious error that demanded correction. Such "correction" could perhaps be undertaken by the court.

The manager seemed to be at a loss in knowing how to deal with the impending discussion and tried to prepare for the worst (as it appeared to him) by enlisting the aid of the head social worker of Mishan. He invited her for a talk and agreed with her that in the meeting she should express opposition to the creation of the court. Her central argument would be the contention that the home is "one big family," in which individuals should relate to each other appropriately and not as if they were part of a bureaucratic society. The manager did not particularly value this social worker, and generally did not pay attention to what she said. Employing her services now was testimony to his sense of powerlessness in the face of the coming confrontation with Mr. Amit. In addition, the manager asked me to contribute a few words about "what science has to say on the subject." Mr. Amit was also very busy preparing for the confrontation. He made the rounds of the home conversing with residents, and making mental notes of possible candidates to be brought "to book."

The meeting was held with the full complement of the group. Other residents who happened to be passing by were asked to leave by the manager, since "this was a closed discussion." The manager was given the floor, and in the course of nearly an hour he disclosed the mainfold annoyances perpetrated by some residents toward their fellows, and the pains taken by him and his staff to maintain standards of cleanliness, aesthetic appearance, and a calm atmosphere within the home. He interrupted his speech to call on the chief maintenance officer to describe a number of incidents in which accepted standards of cleanliness and order had not been observed. The latter devoted most of his contribution to describing the attempts of women residents to bribe the domestics with gifts and money, in order to clean their rooms out of turn before the other rooms. He complained that this interfered with the work schedule. To this the manager added that there was an obviously "unethical" aspect to this state of affairs. At this point, the meeting ended and the discussion about the court was deferred to the following week. In fact, Mr. Amit had decided to end the meeting after the manager had

completed his statement. This fact should be borne in mind in order
to understand the proceedings of the second meeting.

A week later the group reconvened. Mr. Amit opened the discussion by saying that despite the fact that residents often mis-
behave, the home could not be exempted from its part in creating
disorder and related problems. At this the manager interjected that
such comments were not pertinent to the issue (he apparently understood which way the wind was blowing). For his part, Mr. Amit
contended that residents' behavior could not be divorced from that of
the staff and they should be discussed together. Methodically, he
began listing the defects of the home,[13] and stressed two central
issues: the dining room and the service given there ("Worse than a
soup kitchen, we're people, not animals"), and the lack of adequate
medical services. The manager once again interjected, maintaining
that this was hardly his fault, but rather the responsibility of Mishan who refused to allocate the necessary funds. To support his
contention, he mentioned an exchange of letters between himself
and the Mishan head office: "Even Mr. Nahmani (the former secretary of the discussion group) saw the letters and if he were still alive
(he was killed in a road accident) would tell you how much effort I
put into it." This apology was especially striking, in the light of the
animosity that had existed between them in the past. The need to
enlist the late Mr. Nahmani's support denotes the beginning of a
process of abasement that the manager was constrained to undergo
from this point until the end of the meeting.

One after another, the residents rose and told of their suffer-
ings in the home, of defective services, the unsympathetic attitude of
staff, and so on. Every time the manager tried to intervene and
influence the course of the proceedings, he failed. Mr. Amit stressed
that he was running the meeting, and that the manager would be
given an opportunity to respond to the complaints. The manager sat
silently, burying his face in his hands and stopped reacting to what
was being said. When the speakers had spent themselves, he began
to reply, with Mr. Amit pressuring him to limit his remarks. These
amounted, essentially, to a series of apologies and excuses, the main
gist of which was to emphasize his good intentions in the face of the
bureaucratic, budgetary, and personnel problems with which the
home had to contend. He did not try to deny the speakers' complaints, but rather to show that they were directed to the wrong
address. He seemed to realize that denial of what had been said

would only stimulate renewed discussion, possibly even more heated than before. Moreover, in his comments, he hinted to Mr. Amit that he should convey his criticism directly to those people with whom he enjoyed direct contact—the officials of the Mishan directorate. Mr. Amit wanted to hold a vote on the steps to be taken to solve the problems, but the manager requested permission to present to those assembled more "objective" attitudes, as he put it, and asked Mr. Amit to allow the head social worker of Mishan and myself to express our respective viewpoints. Permission was granted. The social worker talked about the need for comradeship and cooperation between the residents whereas I, in very "professional" language, made some vague remarks that could be interpreted in a variety of ways. Mr. Amit's reaction was: "What has been said is important and, so it seems to me, does not undermine my position." In this way, the possible influence of strangers on what was going on was neutralized.

Mr. Amit proposed the establishment of a disciplinary court, stressing that he sought from the group only approval in principle. Once the approval was forthcoming, the group would not be responsible for its activities or mode of operation. This would rest exclusively with the house committee, which would decide on the manner, the composition, and the authority of the body. Things then boiled over, at first there were some incoherent and hesitant whispers and then the muttering increased in volume and words became recognizable: "What arrogant cheek!", "Who does he think he is?" "This isn't the army," "Who put you in charge?" "We don't agree," etc. One of the participants got up and in a voice charged with emotion called on his friends not to vote in favor of the proposal since "in our contract nothing was said about such a court. I want to live according to that contract." Mr. Amit banged the table with the palm of his hand, disciplined the conflicting parties, and called for a vote. The proposal was rejected by a large majority. The manager proposed that the discussion on the creation of the court be delayed until the group members were fully conversant with the problem, and had decided on their views. This proposal was accepted. The manager did not offer a comprehensive counterproposal of his own to Mr. Amit, but he had achieved a postponement of the discussion in a way that did not give Mr. Amit and his supporters a pretext to quarrel with him or claim that he was trying to deny the other residents freedom of choice in their behavior. Mr. Amit closed the meeting and announced that the following discussion would deal with Israeli-Arab relations. He then rose and left the hall.

V

We shall now analyze the process that occasioned the failure of the proposal, by examining how the nature of each stage determined the ensuing stages.

First, a series of general discussions were held on the subject of old age. This was followed by the topic of old-age institutions, with the group expressing support for the manager, who as a result was interested in further discussion of this kind. The session that dealt with the "deviant" residents was nothing more than a logical extension of what had happened before—Mr. Amit was able to impose himself on the direction of all these stages. The discussion on the possibility of establishing a house court was arbitrarily divided by Mr. Amit into two stages. During the first part, a pointed discussion took place about the type of phenomena that such a court was designed to eliminate. But the second part, convened a week after the first, did not contain any reference to the problem under discussion. Instead, it consisted of a series of virulent attacks on the manager and his home—also orchestrated by Mr. Amit. He achieved two objectives by his actions: First, diversion of attention away from the central issue—if the manager had been allowed to continue to raise the issues for discussion, it is conceivable that alternative approaches to the solution of the problem, other than the setting up of the court, would have been conceived of and proposed.

Second, a polarization in the respective stands of the manager and the residents developed. The manager was presented as the accused, as an employee who did not look after the needs of the home as required ("required" according to Mr. Amit—he was presented by the participants in the discussion as responsible for the failures of the institution). Therefore, the conclusion to be drawn was that he was unfit to judge the residents' behavior. This polarization[14] process could have helped Mr. Amit to propose the creation of a disciplinary court based around those residents not subordinate to the manager's authority. At this stage, too, Mr. Amit was in control, giving the floor to some residents, denying others, even the manager. When Mr. Amit proposed the establishment of the court, it was

83

ostensibly intended to represent the end of a planned process, achieving both the isolation of the manager and the enlistment of group members to Mr. Amit's position. After the failure of this proposal, the group returned to consideration of a general subject, Israeli-Arab relations, evidence indeed that the process described above was at least partially planned and the order of the discussion and subject matter was meant to achieve a specific purpose. The manager's moderate proposal facilitated an "honorable retreat" by Mr. Amit, not only by avoiding an open confrontation, but also the continuation of the group's activities in this area. The disintegration of the group seen against the backdrop of the affair of the court could have eroded the position of the manager in the home. The conflict might have become public and gone beyond the bounds of a small group of individuals. Control in such an eventuality would have proved harder to enforce than if the dispute had remained within the discussion group alone. To the outside world, the manager is interested to present the group as living proof of cooperation and agreement between staff and residents. The collapse of this group would have been very deleterious to this aim. In its wake, further personal confrontations between the manager and leaders of the group might have developed, and perhaps even between the manager and the directors of Mishan, with whom the group leaders enjoyed personal ties.

How can Mr. Amit's defeat be explained? It seems that a number of factors may help to provide the answer. Mr. Amit is not considered to be a typical resident. His powerful influence both within and outside the home is well known to the elderly there, and is much greater than that of the other residents. Nor could he have expected them to identify with the idea of a court as a representative governing body of the residents. We should consider his approach to the call for a vote. Mr. Amit did not want the court to operate as an integral part of the discussion group, thus offering to its members the possibility to determine its form. Rather, he viewed the group merely as a means of obtaining a rubber stamp for the implementation of his ideas. The group members realized this was his true aim and were offended. This breakdown in relations between Mr. Amit and the rest of his group served to ostracize him from the framework of loyalties and commitments operative within the group, and thus created a polarization between himself and his colleagues. Despite the fact that formally they all belonged to the same group, the bonds that had formerly helped to make them relatively united no longer existed. So long as Mr. Amit provided subjects for discussion that suited the members of the group, he was assured of their support. However, when he tendered the notion of the establishment of a court that would not be under the jurisdiction of the group, he created a situation in which the members themselves would potentially be subject to Mr. Amit's dictates and their actions constrained by his ideas. In such circumstances, he would be less subject to pressures than the manager himself, and could not be forced to determine the good or bad functioning in accordance with their outside connections (for he would be independent of these connections). Furthermore, Mr. Amit would be able to determine rules of discipline as he saw fit, and the chances of altering them would be relatively slimmer than the possibility of influencing the manager's evaluation. Ironically, it was the very existence of the strong ties that these residents held with the outside that fuelled their objection to the setting up of the court, for Mr. Amit's control would have prevented their exploitation of these connections.

It should be recalled that the residents who took part in the group are well aware of the possibility of contracting various geriatric illnesses, all of which greatly influence the sufferer's behavior. Clearly, some of the "bothersome" residents act as they do because of the effect of such illnesses. It is also known that Mr. Amit has a very intolerant attitude toward this type of "patient." Therefore, there is little doubt that their decision to reject his proposal was colored by these considerations—the possibility of standing powerless before Mr. Amit and his court was much worse than the present situation, in which wide scope is given to manifestation of "deviant" behavior and its evaluation as such when observed. To the aforementioned arguments, we should add the possibility that some of those present weighed up the advantages of supporting Mr. Amit instead of the manager, and concluded that "throwing in their lot" with the latter would reap meaningful rewards in the future (especially since the vote was an open one). For his part, Mr. Amit could not affect the material conditions of life in the home for the residents, and the loss of membership in Mr. Amit's group was weighed against the favors likely to accrue from supporting the manager.

It should be pointed out that a disparity existed between what both Mr. Amit and the manager respectively conceived to be the extent of their power, and the results of the confrontation between them. The manager initially did not believe in his ability to over-come this misfortune (as it seemed to him) and to reject Mr. Amit's proposal explicitly, because "Mr. Amit is a charismatic personality, and the residents will follow him blindly." Despite this, the proposal was rejected. Mr. Amit, on the other hand, was so confident of his ability to realize his aim that he did not even trouble to explain the nature of the court. He expected to receive an unequivocal mandate to establish it, without having to submit to prior investigation and guarantees from the group as to its future operation. He was also mistaken. The source of the mistaken notions of both these individu-als can be located in a single factor—the inability to anticipate possible reactions of the residents due to an insensitivity to their interests and the considerations involved, underpinning these reac-tions. The basis of the relations between group members and Mr. Amit on the one hand, and the manager on the other, was not the product of blind loyalty, or hidden resentment, but concern for the preservation of the best living conditions possible for themselves in the home. The object of this triangular relationship was the lives of other residents in the institution.

The issue of the struggle between Mr. Amit and the manager was that of the authority to control the actions of other residents, actions which, according to Goffman's terminology, constitute in part the "underlife" of the home. The usurpation of the manager's control of the underlife meant the potential loss of one of his sources of power, for until the confrontation with Mr. Amit, his approach to such manifestations had been flexible, depending on which resident was involved and the importance that the manager attached to their actions (this notion will be illustrated in the chapter on the hand-icrafts group). Thus, I would argue that the underlife should be examined not only from the angle of staff-resident relations, but also as part of the network of relations between the residents. The re-sults of the struggle between the manager and Mr. Amit were deter-mined in the main by the state of relations existing among the residents themselves and, perhaps, despite their relations with the manager. The central source of the manager's power—the deter-mination of functioning—cannot be influenced by members of the group. The self-inflicted dissolution of dependence engineered by Mr. Amit between himself and the group was a factor making for his defeat. Apparently, external sources of power may be insufficient,

86

and must be translated into meaningful relations and activities within the institution.

The limits of power enjoyed by both the manager and the residents are conditional not only on their sources, but also on a series of additional factors, such as the facility to activate ties at a particular time, long-term considerations, and specific situations whose special structure can tip the scale decisively.

VI

This analysis of the balance of power involved in the disciplinary court affair throws light only on one aspect of the matter—the nature of manager-resident relationships. However, what occurred during the two meetings described also has implications for the understanding of relations between residents both within and external to the group. In order to convey this idea, an incident will be described that took place during the manager's "abasement" in the discussion on the disciplinary court. Much can be gleaned from this occurrence about the problem of establishing yardsticks for the evaluation of residents' behavior in the home. It has also been broached in the description of the discussion of institutions for the aged that the distinction between those aged who are appropriately placed in the home and those for whom removal is necessary is due mainly to physiological failings. What happens when a resident, who is a member of the group, violates the limits of this sharp distinction through errant behavior?

One of the participants requested the floor in order to complain about the unsympathetic attitude of the staff toward the residents. Mr. Amit gave her permission, and she recounted how one evening while she was watching television she suddenly contracted severe stomach pains and hurried to the toilet. Unfortunately, she was unable to control herself and defecated in the corridor en route. Her neighbors emerged from their rooms, and began to berate her for soiling the place. She asked staff members who happened to be in the vicinity for assistance, but instead they joined in the chorus of reprimand in concert with the other residents. She claimed that this kind of thing could happen to anyone, but here Mr. Amit stepped in, charging her with not sticking to the point. There was dead silence

87

for a moment and then, almost simultaneously, a wave of laughter erupted from those present. The speaker, who had been silenced, burst into tears, yet no one approached to console her. In the next meeting, she was not given the floor at all, although she persistently demanded to speak.

The question arising from this incident is: What was the significance of this laughter? The division into categories of fit and unfit residents involves a sharp differentiation and the varying evaluations applied to everyone are seen to be largely arbitrary. When this categorical division is blurred and someone from the group considered fit shows himself to have behaved like the worst of the vegetables (through lack of control of her bowels), a sharp polarization appears to cut across the two categories, fit and unfit. Moreover, the woman's admission raised the possibility that within the "fit" category lies concealed a category of "unfit," whose manifestations are likely to materialize at any moment (as the woman said before she was interrupted, "This can happen to anyone"). Douglas, in her analysis of the social significance of jokes (1968, 365), notes that the only way to react to such a situation is by laughter, since this merging of categories represents a kind of release from any form of categorization. The breakdown of the physiological barrier by a resident, who belongs to the "wrong" side of this boundary, created a dangerous situation for the group, insofar as it hinted at the possibility of the elimination of this form of categorization and the permeability of one of its foundations—the division between the "bad" and the "good." This is a situation that according to Douglas (1970, 136) may be defined as "pollution." As such, it parallels structurally other situations of pollution, as in the field of religion, and other basic social institutions as well.

Other implications emanating from the court affair can be seen in Mr. Amit's attempt to promulgate rules of behavior and mutual evaluation as he saw fit. The protagonists in the discussion, in spite of their strong external ties, or perhaps because of them, are apparently not yet ready to be governed by a system of rules determined by an individual who is one of their number. For most of them, the manager serves as a kind of administrator who has to accept responsibility for the supply of basic material services (contrary, of course, to the manager's own conception of his role). Mr. Amit, on the other hand, because of his past and his activities within the home, was likely to transform the court into a framework that would fix norms of permissible and impermissible behavior and of good and bad. The creation of such rules would have forced a segment of the fit residents to live in two different worlds, the outside world with which they enjoy ties and the internal world of the institution.

These two pivotal events and their side effects can help us to understand the mechanism underpinning the organization of life in the home for members of the discussion group. Their ties with the outside world aid the processes of internal organization and create for them the possibility of behaving in the home without recourse to special rules or instructions. On the contrary, some of them even raised demands of their own, which were met. For them, the home does not provide a total framework for their lives. Their relations with the manager are based on a recognition of their power and capability and they surmise that he needs their support more than they need him. All of these characteristics indicate that, on the continuum of relative totality, members of the group can be found at the point at which there is an almost complete absence of totality in the institution as far as they are concerned. Sykes (1966, 128–7) describes a similar process in a high-security prison, where a group of prisoners run their lives without hindrance, put other prisoners on trial, and do not obey the guards who fear them. He assumes that this process will be halted because the outside world will not tolerate such a state of affairs. However, it appears that in the old-age home no such outside influence will operate to stop this process, and the nonestablishment of the court came about because of the system of relations between the residents and not with the staff.

From the standpoint of the structure of the relationship, a formal organization, a community that affords the basis for the understanding of comparative totality in the affair of the disciplinary court, facilitates the emergence of the following phenomenon. A resident connected formally with higher-ranking individuals from the standpoint of influence than those who directly "run" the community in which he lives, exploits his links with these high-ranking contacts, in order to impose his will both on other residents and directly on the management of the home. Not only does this resident thus become part of the formal organization, he puts himself in the position of someone who exerts influence in the life of the community. In addition, he also wishes to effect changes within the management structure itself (amounting to a curtailment of its authority), through the exploitation of his own position in the same

89

formal organization for which the management works. Both logically and empirically, this seems to constitute a situation characterized by an almost complete absence of totality. Against this background, the episode of Mr. Amit's defeat is even more striking and the importance of understanding the network of relations operating between residents becomes correspondingly more important.

Another facet of the group's activity is its definition of the condition of the elderly in general, and their subsequent view of the other residents. Two facts may help to understand this phenomenon: the use group members make of physical criteria in distinguishing between various residents in the home, and their attitude toward young people outside the institution. Ostensibly, no connection exists between these considerations. But curiously, it does seem that the answer to the question of why they utilize such physical criteria is rooted in their attitude toward the young. The view of the outside world that the members of the group share is distorted—this is seen by the letters that are sent to international bodies and the high-flown rhetoric to be heard on the values of pioneering, Zionism, morals and so on, without almost any reference to concrete events in the present. Part of this picture is also a function of their attitude towards young people—the tremendous emphasis, with accompanying descriptions of the derision and scorn emanating from the young, derives apparently from the recognition that their yardstick of discrimination between who is or is not old is physical (witness the incident of the old man and the youth). On the one hand, they are upset by the scorn shown to them, and yet on the other, see in the young a focus for positive attitudes, even accepting as valid their criterion for distinguishing between various classes of the elderly. To what extent this standard is arbitrary, and how far they are prepared to adopt it, can be seen in the episode of the woman whose behavior transgressed this categorization and by the insistence of part of the group on the need of removing residents in case of incapacity[15] from the home. It appears that the combination of their special view of the outside world, including the attitude of the young towards them, and the fact of their being lumped together with the ill and the handicapped, helps explain the prominence given to the physical standard for discrimination amongst the elderly.[16]

The interconnections between the recipients of powers (the manager, members of the group, other residents, and the external environment) and the "contours" of the resident's cognitive map become more intelligible in understanding why the concept of functioning is applied. The use of the determination of functioning by the manager as a potential threat to most of the residents does not apply to members of the discussion group but despite this, the concept provides them with a key to the perception of the categorization within the home. Moreover, the prevailing view in the group is that exceptional strictness should be used in applying functioning as the principal differentiating tool in regard to the residents. Their brand of functioning does not bear the broader and more flexible imprimatur of the concept as used by the manager towards the residents, but strips the concept to its formal objective elements before applying it strictly to those residents who fail to meet its exacting physical criteria.

Such a restrictive approach provides the group members with a clear and unambiguous means of structuring the differences between residents. This structuring, which is not subject to negotiation, possesses a static and impartial character and therefore is not given to the manipulation or the penetration of anything less than clear-cut cases. Since the group members believe they will always be defined as functioning well, this rule fulfills a double purpose for them. On the one hand, there is no immediate danger that their deterioration will lead to their removal from the home (unless this is indeed their wish). On the other hand, other residents can be shifted from category to category, and in so doing, provide the background for the "timeless," eternal functioning of the group members.

The situation of controlled change allows the group members to maintain those worlds of meaning relevant to their worldview and identity. The fact that the ethos of the past is not reflected in the reality of the present is counterbalanced by mutual social support in the systems of symbols of the past that they retain. Thus, the power they still retain serves to transform functioning into a tool for sustaining the cognitive categories of the group members. Their own existential dilemma consists of their being old people imbued with a negative self-image. At the same time, their need for a positive, almost mythical self-image is solved by differentiating between old people who function and those who do not, thus setting the members of the group apart from the other old people.

5. THE HANDICRAFTS GROUP

The introduction of occupational therapy into the framework of activities of a total institution or any establishment for economically redundant individuals is a widely accepted and almost taken-for-granted aspect of the attitude towards them and of any treatment program directed at "helping" them. It is also assumed that participation in this sort of handicrafts entails certain standard problems. As payment is usually not made individually and no encouragement is extended to competition between individuals over the quantity and quality of the articles produced, this removes two key motivations to participate. Another factor contributing to the lack of involvement and enthusiasm of the participants is the inability of many to identify with the type of employment in which they are required to engage. The accepted social connection between achievement and social mobility with working life and professional career is patently invalid for occupational therapy. In fact, sometimes there is even a contradiction between an individual's past professional roles and the kind of work in which they are engaged in occupational therapy. This conflict arises mainly in connection with men who were not used to manual work, but who were accustomed to a rigid division of labor between spouses in the family. The feelings of debasement and frustration these men suffer often prevent them from participating actively in the work, and they may show silent or even open resistance to the activity.

In the home studied, the emphasis was shifted from the explicit therapeutic purpose of the activity to the given institutional context, namely the relations between the home and the social system external to it and the problem of functioning. The handicrafts group provides a framework in which the members make articles to be displayed and sold at an annual bazaar open to the public, the proceeds of which are contributed to some public cause.

The questions underlying the description and analysis below will concentrate on the role played by the group as an arena used for demonstrating functioning, on the system of relations between its members and the manager, and on the significance of these relations for structuring the world of those residents who take part in it. Emphasis will be placed in a large degree on differentiation that exists in these relations and the heterogeneity of the members of the handicrafts group.

I

The place of the group in the home, and as a result the meaning of participation in it, can only be understood in the light of the importance of handiwork in the system of perceptions that go to make up the concept of functioning and its implications. In one of our conversations, the manager presented his view of the essence of old age and its problems: "A person is bound to life by various threads, most of which emanate from his work and his relations with colleagues. When he retires a large part of this fabric is cut off, and therefore the home must try to resurrect these ties by means of facilitating employment under its auspices and providing the necessary encouragement to engage in it." It seems to me that the manager largely evaluates the success of his own role in terms of activating residents in the occupational sphere and also on the degree to which his approach approximates the "ideal" type of a homogeneous institution. Evidence of this can be found in his message to the residents as printed in the home's newspaper *The Word of the Fathers*: "I remember the first weeks following the opening of the Home when most of the residents were passive, spending their time not doing anything useful, their single activity being to wait from one meal to the next. Today, a year and a half later, we are able to survey with satisfaction what is being done in the Home. A Soldiers' Welfare Committee has been organized which mobilizes the activities of several dozen people in the workrooms who produce beautiful handiwork, the proceeds of the sale of which are devoted to our soldiers."

The satisfaction about which the manager speaks is directly linked to the establishment of the handicrafts group. Every morning the manager takes up the "mike" in the dining room and addresses the breakfasting residents about the value of work and employment for people in general, and for the elderly in particular. The foundations of this stand towards employment are rooted in several factors.

94

Among the various bodies dealing with care of the elderly, a lively argument is conducted over the best way to assist the elderly individual, be it by placement in a home, heterogeneous or homogeneous, or by the establishment of community day centers.[1] This dispute has a clearly defined economic aspect, which involves the allocation of budgets for the development of institutions or centers of one sort or another. It is clear, therefore, that the manager is interested in demonstrating the positive results of his approach in order to strengthen his position in the argument. The handicrafts group serves to provide him with a source of various sorts of rewards, mainly those deriving from ties with outside elements who are able to support the home by expressions of admiration and encouragement. The handicrafts group achieves this purpose by carrying out exhibitions and sales aimed towards attracting visitors and creating ties with different bodies. When the exhibition and bazaar took place many visitors were invited personally and the event was publicized in various parts of the city. Female volunteers outside the home assisted in the organization of the sale, while the home's residents were asked not to visit for the duration, so as to avoid crowd congestion. The residents were, however, taken on a guided tour by the manager before the formal opening. At the opening itself, a representative of the Soldiers' Welfare Committee spoke and the director of Mishan was also designated to make an address.

Employment for its own sake however is not the only consideration that drove the manager to encourage members of handicraft groups. Testimony to that is the activity of another group, whose members knit for the "Soldiers' Welfare Fund." This group does not hold diverse activities (exhibitions, bazaars) like the handicrafts group. The manager hardly intervenes at all in its operations, despite the praise he extends to it in conversation. In one issue of *The Word of the Fathers*, a number of lines appear that were written by one of the participants of the knitting circle: "In our Home there is a group of women who knit. The value of what they do is incomparably greater than that of others. No one can accuse them of wasting time, for they work in the Home for the benefit of the Soldiers' Welfare Committee. They are always in good spirits and really set a praiseworthy example to others." In this brief paragraph, we see a kind of appeal for attention and recognition similar to that given to members of the handicrafts group, viz. "the value of what they do is incomparably greater than that of others." Moreover, the desire to

95

demonstrate good functioning can be read between the lines: "No one can accuse them of wasting time for they work . . . for the benefit of the Army." In her ensuing remarks, the writer hints at her fear of members leaving the group, and joining the handicrafts group instead. She writes of the great satisfaction to be found in the craft of knitting, and how "it soothes the nerves." A casual acquaintance with these women reveals there is a rivalry, and perhaps even a certain degree of enmity between them and the main handicrafts group. Another point that supports the contention of differential treatment lies in the attitude of the manager towards a number of women who engage in handicrafts purely for their own personal enjoyment—and not for the Soldiers' Welfare Committee. This group, which is housed in a small room adjoining the main handicrafts room, does not attract any interest at all from the manager. He does not bring any visitors or guests to the group, express the slightest praise, nor does he try to persuade other residents to join in.

Yet another factor that appears to shape the manager's attitude in relation to employment derives from his own employment history. Before he assumed his present position, he was responsible for the employment of the disabled in one of the Malben geriatric establishments. Thus, he views his ability to draw as many residents as possible into the sphere of "creative work" (the handicrafts circle) as the measure of his success as manager. He aspires to achieve this, as he explains, "despite the fact that I do not force anyone to work, as is done in Malben, or pay 'workers' a remuneration." His experience in the earlier institution provides a background for his attitude towards the present home, which he expresses in this way: "If you mention my name there you'll find yourself treading on someone's corns. I was always considered to be a nonconformist there, and I'm proud of the fact."

The following paragraphs describe in general terms the key incidents in the development of the group prior to the time of observation. Drawing on this background, we shall trace the formative stages in the relationship between the group and the manager.

A few months after the home opened, one of the residents, Mrs. Levi, began collecting newspapers for the Soldiers' Welfare Committee. She claimed that the manager was not enthusiastic about her activities, and assigned her a place near the dustbins to stack the collected newspapers. However, after the Soldiers' Welfare Committee praised her efforts, the manager relented somewhat and allowed her to use the security rooms that are located on every floor as collection points. Mrs. Levi then decided to broaden her activities on behalf of the committee. She proposed to Mrs. Shimoni, her friend, to set up of a group of women who would engage in handicrafts, sell the articles produced, and contribute the proceeds to the Soldiers' Welfare Committee. Mrs. Shimoni, who had been very active in the life of the home since its inception and had a large circle of friends, managed to recruit a group of about ten women, most of them of Bulgarian extraction, who then based themselves in a specially designated handicrafts room containing work tables, looms, sewing machines, cupboards, and other equipment. Up to that time, little use had been made of the room except for a few women who undertook private sewing work.

The group received no financial assistance from the management and the women purchased the raw materials required at their own expense. As the group grew, the handicrafts room became a hive of activity, so that the manager decided the directorate should support it. In the autumn of 1971, a fair took place to sell the group's products. Many guests were invited to the celebration, drawn mainly from the ranks of the relatives of residents, staff, and those in different disciplines involved in dealing with the problems of old age. The handicraft sale was very successful, bringing in an income of IL.10,000, with IL.8,000 (about 6500$ and 4500$) donated to the Soldiers' Welfare Committee. The balance was used to buy raw materials and equipment for future use. A representative of the Soldiers' Welfare Committee thanked the contributors and presented the home with a certificate of appreciation that was hung in a conspicuous location on the wall, and that every visitor to the home was brought to see. The ceremony and the certificate were a source of pride to the directorate, and particularly to members of the group. The fair provided the home with a great deal of publicity, mainly amongst other old-age homes, and the manager, together with the women of the group, decided to continue the project and to organize another fair the following year, since its great success had turned the handicrafts group into a focus of interest in the home. Within a few months more women joined and products began to be sold on a piecemeal basis outside the fair framework, to tourists and visitors. Various contributors now started to supply many raw materials, and even investigated the possibility of selling the products commercially (this never materialized). The directorate began to employ a paid sewing instructress, who worked throughout the group's working hours—from 9:00—11:00 (am) daily. It seems clear the manager's interest in the group and the importance he attached to it began when the group provided him with a source of contact with the outside world.

//

As far as the number of participants is concerned, three periods may be distinguished: the pre-bazaar phase, with between ten to fifteen individuals, the phase after the first bazaar with some thirty, and the period of January to May 1972 with again around fifteen participants.

With the passage of time, the group crystallized into a number of different, distinct social clusters: Mrs. Shimoni's group, the "loners," the teacher, and Mr. Nachmani. Despite engaging in similar activities such as handiwork, its significance was different for Mrs. Shimoni's group of women on the one hand, and for the loners on the other. We will examine what the results were of the activity within the group for all its constituent factions. The questions to be posed in this regard are: What are the relations between the participants and the manager? How are the relations affected by the residents' power base both within and outside the home? The argument that we will try to develop is that among participants occupied in the same activity, it is possible to discern different levels of exchange relations, so that the pattern of participation serves as a model for the differential distribution of power within the home.

Mrs. Shimoni, who was one of the group's founders, gathered together ten women, most of whom she had developed a relationship with before the group had been established. She acted as an intermediary between the group and the manager. This mediation manifested itself in the organization of visitors coming to observe the work of the group, and in the determination of what would be exhibited in the next bazaar. But principally, her importance was made apparent in her ability to elicit favors for her friends, such as a move from one double room to another—one of the most intractable problems faced by residents—or in obtaining improved personalized care and cleaning service from the house mother, and so on. Membership in Mrs. Shimoni's group ensured protection against the possibility of a negative evaluation of their functioning. It should be recalled that most of the women participants were dependent on the group and its activities. An example of this dependence was Mrs. Kohavi, a participant and close friend of Mrs. Shimoni, who never stopped complaining about the home, its employees, and especially the manager. She did this in an uninhibited fashion. One morning the manager paid a visit, together with the head social worker of Mishan. When they approached the table at which Mrs. Shimoni and Mrs. Kohavi were working, the latter began to engage the social worker in conversation, and within the earshot of the manager, protested that "this [place] is far from being the paradise he [the manager] would have you believe. Just this morning the gatekeeper told me he'll be glad when I die. Nobody really cares, the place is dirty, the work is boring and the residents are a nasty lot." Mrs. Shimoni tried unsuccessfully to silence her. The social worker stood there aghast, and the manager could not even react. Afterward, in his office, the latter dismissed the incident, explaining that "Mrs. Kohavi is crazy, don't listen to her." With this the subject was closed. Despite conforming to all his criteria for "poor functioning" and thus being a candidate for removal from the home, the "crazy" Mrs. Kohavi's position was not threatened by the manager.

The dependence of members of the group on Mrs. Shimoni was enhanced by the kind of products made and the nature of the work itself. Mrs. Shimoni's colleagues specialized in comparatively simple work and provided useful articles (babies' clothing, skirts, etc.). Since she organized the allocation of work, Mrs. Shimoni determined who would do what and when. She provided the materials, gave advice, and all this—given the type of handicrafts being produced—made the dependence on her decisions all the greater. In the group's eyes, the success of the exhibition of work was their dominant aspiration, for the exhibition provided them with an objective measure of evaluation for their work. The achievement of a high price for any particular product became a status symbol for the worker who produced it. Thus, a common interest existed between the manager and Mrs. Shimoni's group regarding the viability of the "sale." Any interference with this cooperation might undermine the ability of members of the circle to exploit their position in it, in order to gain positive evaluation and favors from the manager. Mrs. Shimoni was proud of her good relations with the manager. Repeated references to these relations reinforced the dependence of the group on her. She was the only resident allowed to keep sewing equipment and a cupboard for accomodating it in her room, and she didn't fail to lay stress on this privilege. Mrs. Shimoni was one of the few residents whom the manager introduced to visitors and with whom he recommended that they speak. In these talks, she lavished praise on the home and claimed, for example, that "no resident lived and functioned so well before he entered the home". The fact that the group offered a medium for the demonstration of proper functioning, and that Mrs. Shimoni maintained good relations with the manager, made her coworkers dependent on her because she mediated between what went on in the group and the manager. This mediating ability and the dependence of the group on Mrs. Shimoni gave it an important bargaining position vis-à-vis the manager.

Mrs. Shimoni tried as far as possible to settle quarrels and to smooth things over when any sort of difference of opinion arose. Even when Mrs. Kohavi claimed that her wish to change rooms had been refused because "the manager hates me as I'm a Sephardi," Mrs. Shimoni replied quietly that she was also a Sephardi, but the manager certainly did not hate her, to which the complainant said definitely: "Yes, it's true you're a Sephardi, but you have a special pull with the manager." Mrs. Shimoni rejoined quietly that she would try to take the matter up with the manager (thus endorsing the claim of special "pull" with him). When further provocations failed to elicit a response, the one-sided argument died of its own accord. The effort to preserve group unity, even at the cost of a personal insult, attested to Mrs. Shimoni's conviction that the source of her power and esteem emanated from the group. Undermining or dissolution of the group was liable to endanger both her status in the group (and, by implication, also in the home) and her main talent—the facility to organize and lead.

Within the group itself, there was a nucleus of two women closer to Mrs. Shimoni than the others. In contrast, another larger subgroup was not considered by the other members to belong to the group at all, even though they themselves disputed this. A recurring incident that illustrates this internal structure concerns the distribution of refreshments. At 11:00 A.M., after most of the loners have left the room and only Mrs. Shimoni and her instructress remain, one of the participants prepares a soft drink for Mrs. Shimoni and her two friends and asks some of the others if they would also like a drink. Those whose membership of the group is not universally accepted are not asked at all. Usually they overlook the insult and individually request refreshment, which is given. It seems they were seeking to demonstrate their sense of belonging to the group in this fashion—the privilege of getting a drink had come to symbolize this belonging.

Activity in Mrs. Shimoni's group was not confined to handicrafts, but also included random conversations held during and between working sessions. These conversations included the exchange of information about what was going on in the home and gossip about other residents, but their principal content was that of self-congratulation. This type of social exercise was not concerned with the nature of the articles produced or the anticipated profit from their sale, but related to their position in the home as a result of their participation in the group. Expressions like "We're like the intelligentsia of the home" refer to the group most respected by the women of the handicrafts group—the discussion group. These comparisons with the discussion group included arguments on the importance of education in "getting ahead" and on the value of participation in various cultural activities, but were principally concerned with incidents from the history of the settlement of the country and with public activity. Most of these women had not enjoyed special ties with public bodies, and their occupational status (they had been housewives, clerks, etc.) clearly indicated that they did not belong to the same circles as the members of the discussion group. Despite this, they were particularly sensitive about the use of Hebrew, although most were Ladino-speakers, and prided themselves on their children's and grandchildren's achievements at universities and other educational institutions.

In conversation, when asked to talk about their past lives, many took pains to look for some indication of Zionist or community activity, and elevated this to be the focal point of their conversation,[2] like Mrs. Shimoni who recalled her early schooldays in her native Bulgaria and participation in a small Zionist group there. When the folklore circle asked her to describe her hometown and its customs, she concentrated her remarks on that same group, while broadening the subject to include the yearning of Bulgarian Jews to emigrate to Israel and their efforts to realize this goal. Another participant pointed out that her late husband had been very active in the Zionist movement and had died as a result of his involvement.

The attitude of the women in the group toward nonparticipant residents was also based on this standard of evaluation. The latter were variously called "senile," "idiots," "not right in the head," and the harshest epithet of all, "animals," the last used to describe the facial expressions of those residents who spent their time sitting around the lobby: "This one looks like a horse, that one a donkey, and the one over there in the corner a pig," and so on. All these nicknames denote intellectual and cognitive denigration. The epithet "animal," in addition to dehumanizing the resident (as do the "vegetable" and "exhibition" categorizations used by the members of the discussion group and by staff) by stressing his physiological determination, is primarily intended to indicate changes in his mental state. The nickname "vegetable" denotes a reduction in or absence of mobility, which is a physiological trait. In contrast, the word "animal" and the attribution of the facial expressions of various animals indicates an animalistic quality—namely, a low level of intellectual activity. Why did this standard develop in Mrs. Shimoni's group? It seems that the answer lies in the way the women in the group saw the "human pyramid" of the home, with members of the discussion group characterized by their intellectual gifts at the pinnacle, and at the base, the animals, with the complete absence of those qualities. This is where the intellectual standard originates and the source of the emphasis placed on this kind of activity in the group. The respect accorded to members of the discussion group is even more striking when viewed in terms of the very superficial personal ties they enjoy with them, and the (perceived) wide cultural divide separating the two groups. It was this very absence of close acquaintance with Mr. Amit and his friends that allowed the members of the handicrafts group to create a halo around those supremely wholesome individuals who were worthy of unquestioning emulation. For them, no distinction existed between the national symbols as exemplified by the personalities comprising the discussion group and their personal traits. From this standpoint, the home has not distorted the system of categories that shape the attitude of members of the group to this aspect of the national pantheon.

III

The handicrafts group included some participants who were not necessarily interested in participating in the fair, and who did not maintain close ties with each other. These individuals can be divided into two categories, according to the reasons they see for their being in the home. The first subgroup enjoys their social participation in the group, while the others obtain personal satisfaction primarily from their work, with involvement in the group being a secondary consideration for them. The number of such "loners" was not fixed, varying from five to ten individuals.

The first category included individuals who felt that as a result of their very unstable health and lack of integration in the life of the home, as well as the absence of outside connections, they were liable to be expelled from the institution.

During the daily morning round of the manager, it was possible to see them engrossed in their tasks and demonstrating great industry. The manager sometimes came up to them and exhorted them with a few words of praise. On one such visit the manager had invited the chief social worker of Mishan. He paused for a while beside one of the men who was plaiting a basket and praised his perseverance. After the visit, the manager explained to the guest that the man, despite his handicap and precarious health, proved by his actions that occupational activity succeeds in "keeping a person going." What the manager did not know, however, was that after his visit the man disappeared, returning to the group only on the following morning in anticipation of the manager's next "tour" (it took place at 9:30, shortly after the opening of the workroom). The rest of those present were aware of the basketmaker's strange custom and excused his behavior by referring to his perilous state of health. As one of Mrs. Shimoni's ladies put it: "He needs to show that he can work, and all credit to him." In conversation, the man admitted that he "hates this tedious work," but failed to elaborate on why he persevered with it.

Another example can be seen in the case of a sickly woman who had lost one of her arms but still participated in the group despite the fact that "the windows are closed and I suffocate, and it's hard for me to work with one hand." Moreover, she knew that her work would not find its way into the exhibition—confirmation of which she had received from Mrs. Shimoni. In addition, she had cataracts in both eyes and sewing proved to be a strain for her. During the last few months she had visited her sons up in the North a great deal and had even slept over. She stressed that she was the widow of a physician who had "devoted his life to the country and was a genuine idealist." These frequent visits may have been designed to serve as a sort of preparation for developing potential support in the event that she would be forced to leave the home one day. Her declarations of belonging to "the generation of founding fathers", evoked a deep feeling in her and in others of affinity with members of the discussion group for whom no threat of expulsion existed. It seems that the fear of being expelled pushed her to operate in several directions simultaneously, each direction complementing the others. At least as far as the handicrafts group was concerned, these efforts were worthwhile—she received a great deal of praise, both openly and behind the scenes, for her efforts. Mrs. Shimoni and the manager both drew the attention of visitors to the group to the fact that "willpower enables anything to be achieved notwithstanding physical handicap." Thus, the manager was able to present further evidence to substantiate his position. The fact that this woman did not use the group for purely social purposes supported his contention that members of the group did not make up her social circle.

Until now, I have tried to clarify a number of factors bearing on the participation of residents in the handicrafts group, seeking to demonstrate good functioning in order to resolve a central existential problem facing them: continuation of their residence in the home and improvement of their self-image in the eyes of others as well.

The second category of loners included disparate individuals who shared only a common desire to derive personal satisfaction from their handicraft activities, irrespective of the group itself and its place in the home. Thus, their presence in the group was a product of personal idiosyncracies, and the meaning of their actions should be understood within this framework. Two such cases will now be described.

A woman who had been married to a well-known artist, and had subsequently divorced him a number of years before, claimed that she had always wanted to involve herself with the world of art not only passively (visits to exhibitions, showing interest) but also creatively. Preoccupation with being a wife and mother had taken up most of her time, and only now, when her time was her own, was she free to explore her own creativity. Her artistic pursuits found expression on the walls of her room, which were decorated with many pictures, with frequent visits to exhibitions, and in random conversation with anyone interested in hearing about artistic trends and concerns. She came to the work room after the manager's daily visit—when the atmosphere was more relaxed and the crowding was more tolerable, throwing herself into her work rather than conversing with the rest of the participants. Her embroidery creations were intricate and complicated, winning her admiration and inspiring wonderment from all who saw them. This kind of work relied heavily on materials and tools and required a large working area, and therefore could not be performed in the confines of her room or anywhere else other than the handicrafts room. She said old age had confronted her with her most serious crisis, because all her life she had been accustomed to an aesthetic and pleasing environment. Now, she felt, she was obliged to be party to a process of progressive ugliness in herself, and in the human environment around her. She thought the main advantage of a home for the elderly was its relative isolation from "healthy, beautiful people who always make me recall my youth, as contrasted with my situation today." She attributed her preoccupation with art, among other factors, to the social isolation to which she had sentenced herself: "Art allows me to realize myself." This is a case in which the battle against change is waged privately, without resort to the help of others to forge the tools of functioning.

The second case involved a man who had never engaged in handicraft work before. A short while before, his wife had died suddenly in his presence. He was in shock for many months, remaining mute and fearful in a self-imposed isolation. His doctors advised him to enter an old-age home, where he would find company and occupational activity that would relieve his grief and anxiety. He followed this advice, was accepted into the home, and began to participate in the group "just to keep busy and forget my troubles for at least a few hours." His choice of handicraft was the hard, demanding work of rug weaving—requiring a great deal of concentration, and it enabled him, he claimed, to take his mind off his sorrow. He did not bother to converse with others in the group. This man had two married sons in senior government positions, and they had arranged for him to be placed in the home very quickly. It is therefore reasonable to assume that for him the group did not serve as a source of achieving status in the eyes of the manager and the other residents.

What then were the relations between the loners and Mrs. Shimoni's group? In order to clarify this, a description of the type of products made by the loners is necessary. Two products were described above, and the rest do not differ too much from them in substance, being principally petite point work, small-scale carpet making, embroidery, and so on. The work requires relatively uniform materials (mainly embroidery and weaving thread), and a few tools that do not require replacement. The work itself takes a long time to complete, compared to the production of other articles. Continuous instruction and guidance is not required. The products are mainly decorative, and therefore do not have to adapt to others or fit. All of these characteristics mean there is a minimal dependence of the producer on materials, instruction, or future stages of work—in contrast to the work supervised by Mrs. Shimoni and her instructresses. Thus, a situation was created in which there was no pretext, occupationally, for communication between the loners and Mrs. Shimoni, and as was mentioned earlier, there was no contact in any other sphere. The separation between the two types of participants was so marked that occasionally Mrs. Shimoni's "women" openly gossiped about the loners in their presence, and referred to them as if they were nonentities. All this occurred, however, without eliciting any response from the other side.

A curious incident offers proof that even in the absence of a reaction, the loners were aware of what was going on in the group, and if the opportunity arose to exploit the situation for their own advantage, they would do so. One morning the conversation in Mrs. Shimoni's group turned on the situation of residents in double rooms who were unmarried. In this context, one of the loners whose roommate persecuted her and caused her much anguish was mentioned. At first the victim did not react, but after several minutes had been devoted to an extensive coverage of her woes by the others, she got up from her place, joined the conversation, and added many more details, saying that "if you could tell the manager about all this it might help"—after which she returned to her place. This departure from the usual pattern of conversation offers clear evidence of the loners awareness of Mrs. Shimoni's ability to influence the manager.

These patterns of participation represent three degrees of dependence. The loners who use the group as a medium of demonstrating good functioning are the most highly dependent, and the sphere of meaning accorded to their activity is determined correspondingly. Mrs. Shimoni's subgroup has power in its own right—in its relations with the manager—and its members see more than a medium for the demonstration of functioning. From this standpoint, the extent of their dependence is less than for the first group. It is a mutual dependence that is anchored in "give and take" relations, and the bargaining positions held by both sides. The loners who participate in the group for personal reasons, wholly unrelated to functioning, represent, at least so far as group activity is concerned, an almost complete absence of dependence, and the sphere of meaning of their participation does not touch upon relations with the manager.

Mrs. Shimoni's group and the loners are residents who engage in handiwork. In addition to them, there is a paid instructress, whose real profession is occupational therapy. She never alludes to this fact, and her function in the group is expressed mainly in helping the loners by providing materials and instruction. She remains aloof from Mrs. Shimoni's field of operations and, like her, is interested in the success of the exhibition, through which she is able to show publicly the results of her instruction.

We can better understand the group as a medium for negotiations between the manager and the residents with the aid of a description and analysis of the dynamics of a particular system of social relations, which in many respects differed from the norm. This case history shows both the connections between the group and other organizations in the home, as well as the interplay among various power sources, and their manipulation, as reflected in one particular episode.

IV

A description of the group's history makes clear the shifts in the manager's attitude to the group over time as well as the alterations in types of cooperation between him and the participants. These changes were manifested in the direction of an increasing involvement by the manager in the affairs of the group. This interference furnishes an example of the dynamic aspect of dependency relations, whose degree is determined as a result of contacts, some of them being struggles in the course of time between the manager and the residents. This point will be clarified in reference to an explanation of the state of relations between the manager and Mr. Nahmani, who played a central role in the handicrafts group.

Everyone mentioned until now stressed, to a greater or lesser extent, the success of the bazaar as the key factor in their activity, in consonance with the manager's wishes. It is in this light that discussion of the relations between Mr. Nahmani and the manager must be understood.

Mr. Nahmani was one of those residents with "his finger in every pie." From his very first day in the home he revealed wide-ranging interests and displayed activity in many different fields. He worked in the manager's office. He conducted correspondence with the social security office on behalf of those residents who had problems with that body. He managed to secure exemption from payment of the television license fee for residents. Despite not being religious, he was the first secretary of the synagogue, and in this capacity arranged suitable furnishings and equipment for it. Until his death, he was the secretary of the discussion group, kept the minutes, and was responsible for distributing invitations to its meetings. He also participated in the drama circle, and assisted in the setting up and efficient organization of other groups. He knew most of the residents and their problems personally. He addressed everyone benevolently, and always had a kind, pertinent, and friendly word to make to everyone. (In the elevator: "Hello, Mrs. Hava, I see you're keeping up your gym classes. Excellent, you look great.") In general, the residents were very fond of him, as can be seen in a reference to him in *The Word of the Fathers*, in which he was the recipient of a special greeting as follows: "To Mr. Nahmani, beloved by all—may he flourish in good health and find the energy to continue his friendship and assistance to anyone who is in need, and may he also be blessed with success in his recently revealed acting talent."

Mr. Nahmani joined the handicrafts group immediately after the inaugural bazaar. In characteristic fashion, he began organizing energetically and efficiently the group's activities. He himself did not do handicraft work (although he had been a manual worker for most of his life). Instead, he concentrated on putting the group's accounts in order—mainly as a result of the bazaar—by purchasing equipment and raw materials, and completing an inventory of the articles for sale in the next bazaar. He also accepted responsibility for fund-raising from contributors and sales alike, as well as for the disbursement of funds for the group's needs, thus controlling the group's purse strings. All financial transactions were noted in a school exercise book that he took around with him wherever he went, and which he refused to show to anyone. The manager encouraged his activities and actually gave him a free hand, and Mr. Nahmani reciprocated by helping the manager to overcome, in large measure, administrative problems both internally and in regard to the outside world.

His relations with Mrs. Shimoni were good. They divided the organizational work between them, in order to eliminate any sources of friction or argument that might arise. Mr. Nahmani dealt mainly with relations with different bodies outside the group, while Mrs. Shimoni, as described earlier, dealt principally with management of the group itself.

During the winter of 1972, the number of participants in the handicrafts room declined. This was as a result of a quarrel between Mrs. Shimoni and one of the other founders of the group. The formation of Mrs. Shimoni's subgroup had led to the isolation of this woman. She reacted by organizing a circle of women workers, based in their rooms outside the handicrafts room, but within the framework of the group—thus allowing their participation in the bazaar. Mrs. Shimoni demanded the manager to do something to increase the number of participants in the group, claiming that otherwise the success of the bazaar might be jeopardized. The manager reacted by exploiting Mrs. Shimoni's wish to enlarge her area of control in terms of the rivalry between her and her colleague. (This conflict was only one of many in the history of Mrs. Shimoni's involvement with the group, all of which had until then resulted in her success to resist the encroachment of her competitors and, in fact, ejecting them completely from the group.) The manager took action, which he claimed was intended to serve that purpose, but in reality was directed against Mr. Nahmani.

Mr. Nahmani, who considered himself responsible for all the group's activities, did not support Mrs. Shimoni's contention about the danger to the success of the bazaar. Indeed, his records showed a rise in "production." Despite the evidence, the manager decided to refer the subject of the handicrafts group to the discussion group for debate, although under a different heading. During a subsequent group meeting, Mr. Amit announced, to his regret, that lately rumors were abroad in the home to the effect that deficiencies existed in the administration of the handicrafts group, and consequently some residents demanded some form of investigation. He did not specify either accused or accusers, but it was clear that what he said was aimed at Mr. Nahmani. He also noted that the number of participants was dropping, and it was necessary to take steps to ensure the success of the forthcoming bazaar. He therefore proposed giving "a more formal dimension to the group's activities," so as not to aid its detractors, by establishing a supervisory watch committee from amongst those members of the discussion group who did not participate in the handicrafts group. A body would be elected to run its affairs, which would include its own members, and in which there would be a clear-cut division of functions. In this way, a body of rules could be formulated as guidelines for future activity. These proposals were accepted unanimously, on the spot, and a watch committee was chosen that would supervise the management of the handicrafts group, the purchase of materials, sales, and the account-keeping. Mr. Nahmani was asked to convene a special meeting of the women of the group, during which a management committee would be elected, and this was what in fact took place. Mr. Nahmani (chairman), Mrs. Shimoni, her rival, and four other residents were so elected. It was decided that only the management would be responsible for matters affecting the sales of products, purchase of raw materials and equipment for the handicrafts room—all of which had been up till then the sole prerogative of Mr. Nahmani. Furthermore, Mr. Nahmani was now asked to keep a precise record of materials, equipment, articles produced, who made what, and how long it took.

In order to understand what happened at that meeting of the discussion group, two things must be made clear:

First, there is almost no doubt that raising the subject of the handicrafts group at the meeting was preceded by a decision taken by the house committee.[3] One of the members of this group, the vice-chairman of the discussion group, claimed that one of the main topics for discussion was the question of occupation for the residents and, in particular, placement in the handicrafts group.

Second, regarding rumors, the spreading of rumors and gossip in the home is an everyday fact of life. Men and women congregate in different corners of the entrance hall and talk about what is going on in the home and about fellow residents, so that the circulation of rumors about the handicrafts group, if indeed this occurred, is not extraordinary. It should be noted that in the group itself, nobody had mentioned such rumors before the meeting of the discussion group. After details of that meeting were made known, I heard about these rumors from Mrs. Shimoni's rival. She did not specify that their source was the discussion group, but presented them as facts.

110

Thus, she said: "There are rumors that things are amiss in the group. Residents are even saying that stealing goes on, but I don't subscribe to that." For our purposes, what is important is the use of the rumors made by the discussion group and their exploitation as a pretext to encroach on Mr. Nahmani's special preserve.

Mr. Nahmani was placed in a difficult position. Open opposition to the discussion group's decision would have put him on a collision course with the group, with whom he aspired to full membership (he was almost the only member of the group who had not joined because of his personal outside connections or by virtue of his past public activity, but rather because of his contributions and standing within the home). He did not react during the discussion. Subsequently, he became part of the new, more formal administration of the handicrafts group. His explanation of what took place was as follows: "In order to make the group official, and thus to attract more residents, the imprimatur of the management was necessary." Despite his disregard of the protest that brought about the discussion, it is clear from his comments that Mr. Mahmani was aware of two aspects of the situation: a) the problem of functioning—where residents are drawn into activities endorsed by the management, and b) the fact that the handicrafts group now had become more fully integrated into the home, in the sense that the management was the primary influence on what occurred within the group.

The impression that the proceedings in the discussion group had been mainly directed at Mr. Nahmani was strengthened by the two actions that the manager took immediately following the decision of that group.

First, the keys of the handicrafts room were taken away from Mr. Nahmani so that he could not open up the room at will, as in the past. This step prevented Mr. Nahmani from bringing visitors or potential buyers to the room, and curtailed his ability to develop ties with contacts outside the home. In response to this, he transferred the focus of his activity in the group to his room. There he kept his records and notebooks, and there he even began to receive various people connected with the group such as suppliers of equipment and materials.

Second, the accounting procedures were taken away from Mr. Nahmani, and split among three other individuals. It is useful to take a look at these people in order to understand why the manager nominated them, what they could contribute to the handicrafts

111

group, and what their standing in the home was. The first man (chronologically) appointed to the group's management team received the authorization to sign checks for the purchase of materials and equipment. This resident had been the owner of a carpet factory, and still maintained ties with suppliers of weaving materials. He mobilized these connections for the benefit of the group, receiving materials at reduced prices. The second man, elected to the management group, was granted control of the petty cash float for small, day-to-day purchases. The third individual was not formally elected, but assumed the function of chairman of the inspection committee on behalf of the discussion group. He was asked in writing, by Mr. Amit, to check the accounts of the handicrafts group. Subsequently, he joined the management group, and began keeping the accounts.

In order to understand the status of this last individual in the system of relations between the group and the manager, some aspects of his role in the home and activities should be noted. He had worked thirty-two years as a floor manager in a factory manufacturing sewing thread, and retired at the age of seventy-two. At that time, he was engaged in a great deal of public service work. He served as bookkeeper and treasurer for the local W.I.Z.O (the Womens International Zionist Organization) branch for a nominal salary, and as honorary president and member of the executive of a local charitable fund, as well as being responsible for its disbursements. He spent a great deal of time in town and had a circle of friends based outside the home. It seems clear, therefore, that he did not regard the home to be the center of his world. The bookkeeping for the group was something of a marginal activity for him, and almost the only one he conducted within the home. His isolation from the social life of the group and the home and his ties with the manager and the leaders of the discussion group made him a contributory factor in the strengthening of the institutional "hold" over the handicrafts group. Evidence for this can be adduced from a new function he assumed in the group—the collection of contributions from the residents on behalf of the group. The one-dimensional character of his relations with the other residents found its sole expression in this task, enabling him to separate this function from others, and thus to perform it more effectively. The absence of social relations with other residents limited his freedom of maneuver in his dealings with the manager. He certainly did not enjoy the wide circle of acquaintances, contacts, activities, and admiration in the home that Mr. Nahmani had. Taking the manager's advice, this person recruited someone outside the group to help him keep a personal index on suppliers, details of when work projects started, were completed, and so on. This index enabled the manager to keep track of the work activities within the group according to criteria already known to him from his work in Malben. With the aid of this information, he could also apprise himself of the functioning of members of the group, and thus urge some of them to work harder, a stratagem that would increase the number of articles produced and the success of the bazaar. It appears that the choice of these three men to manage the group was very deliberate. This notion is supported by the many entreaties made to them to actually become members of the group, with all that this entailed.

The nature of the confrontation between Mr. Nahmani and the manager can be clarified only if we understand the latter's perception of Mr. Nahmani. As mentioned before, the manager had been at Malben, and had resigned because, as he said: "I would not agree to turn a person into a number and constrain him to work." He regarded himself as a nonconformist, who was opposed to an intellectualized approach to his work, preferring the "personal touch." As an example of this attitude, he cited the affair of his relations with Mr. Nahmani. In his own words:

> When Mr. Nahmani actually began to live in the home, I knew about his poor work relations in the past, and that he was a difficult and stubborn individual. Despite this, I appointed him secretary of the synagogue, where he promptly quarreled with the rabbi and treasurers, and voices were raised. I called him in for a talk, and for over an hour he told me about himself and his desires. I realized that this was a man bent on achieving power and control at the top of the ladder, and unprepared to see himself as one among equals. I decided to use this weakness for the home's benefit, and appointed him to the post of manager of the handicrafts group. I knew that in this position he would not be confronted with any rivalry, and this would satisfy his needs and he would be useful to everyone. It turned out like this. Mr. Nahmani did the work of three men, and I gave him a free hand, even though he wasn't always right. Some residents were sympathetic to him, many were hostile,

113

although they didn't show it. After his death in a road accident, I divided up his duties amongst three individuals, and now things are proceeding smoothly. His death was indeed sudden, but even so, we are back on course in our preparations for the exhibition and sale of work.

During the same conversation, although in another context, the manager told me about the job offers he had received after he left Malben, and of his refusal to work in a private institution despite the tempting salary. He said: "I can't have my cake and eat it. In a private institution, I'm subject to the desires and financial demands of the backers, while here I can do as I please and no one interferes in my dealings with the residents." These remarks and his comments about Mr. Nahmani do not suffice to explain his relationship with the latter, but a number of points can be gleaned from them about its nature. First, the manager entirely ignored the events that took place in the discussion group, and misrepresented their results (". . . after his death I divided up his job among three people"). Second, he tried to belittle the image of Mr. Nahmani as a central figure, much admired in the home. He spoke of his enemies and quarrels (about which I did not hear from any other source), and contended that everything was proceeding smoothly after Mr. Nahmani's death. Third, he referred to Mr. Nahmani's desire for power as a negative characteristic, and described it as a "weakness," while simultaneously alluding to his own desire for the same with the opportunity for unfettered control of the residents. Fourth, he stressed his intention to use Mr. Nahmani for the home's benefit and of directing his energies into channels he thought desirable. The manager's position here, toward Mr. Nahmani, is very similar to that adopted by the discussion group, when it, too, took steps to limit his authority. Unlike the affair of the disciplinary court, the manager did not describe Mr. Nahmani's power as charismatic and unbridled, as he had done in Mr. Amit's case. The explanation for this can be found in the different power base of the two residents. Mr. Amit drew most of his power from his close ties with influential institutions and individuals outside the home, over whom the manager had no control, and of whose nature he did not have exact information. In Mr. Nahmani's case, the situation was different, for here the manager defined the problem clearly and decisively. He saw Mr. Nahmani as a power-drunk individual who needed to be

114

curbed. The means for enforcing control and restraint were at his disposal, and he indeed made use of them. This situation derived from the fact that Mr. Nahmani's power emanated exclusively from his contacts within the home. These relations could be determined at their source and so undermined, thus harming Mr. Nahmani's standing. It seems, at least in this case, that the concept of charisma served as a label for those sources of influence that were insufficiently defined and, moreover, which the defining agent had no practical possibility of harnessing directly for his ends.

Goffman (1961a, 16) speaks of a process of "adjustment," by which the resident adapts to his institutional context, as perceived by the staff. It appears that the manager's actions against Mr. Nahmani were part of this process, designed to achieve the adjustment of a resident wielding power and showing initiative, and at the same time, to control one of the groups in the home more efficiently. Since this process is not one-sided, but accompanied the reactions of the adjusted resident, we will try to trace some of Mr. Nahmani's responses to these new circumstances.

Mr. Nahmani, feeling that his wings had been clipped in the handicrafts group, redirected his energy and interest into another field. He began to try to organize lectures in the home. He wanted to bring in various lecturers who would address themselves mainly to the problems of old age and thus "aid the residents to comprehend their situation and perhaps teach them ways of overcoming it and enriching their spiritual life." The issuing of invitations to lecturers was the prerogative of the manager, and had it not been for Mr. Nahmani's untimely death, this incursion into the manager's territory would have placed him in yet another direct confrontation with the management.

In the handicrafts group itself, Mr. Nahmani spent less time than he had prior to the discussion. Even during the short periods he spent in the handicrafts room, he avoided organizational or managerial tasks, but preferred to take part in simple auxiliary work such as arranging tools or sorting out threads. The focal point of his activity was now centered around the instructress. Mr. Nahmani helped her to distribute materials, in the collection of tools from the participants, and their preparation for further use. In the course of these activities, Mr. Nahmani had opportunities to engage in conversation and to exchange ideas with the instructress, and indeed their relationship flourished until his death. The result of the deliberations of the discussion group was to transfer control of the handicrafts group to a collection of individuals, of whom only some were known to the instructress through her work in the handicrafts room. The others (the accountant and his aides) were outside her field of contacts in the group, and therefore no chance existed that dual relationships of mutual dependence would develop between them, such as those that had existed with Mrs. Shimoni. In fact, the instructress was dependent for the supply of materials and equipment on the management of a group that was now cut off from her. Mr. Nahmani, now the official chairman of the management, was the person with whom the instructress had previously enjoyed a relationship. On this basis, she could develop new ties and strengthen the existing ones. The basis of Mr. Nahmani's interest in these contacts with the instructress was more involved. Apparently, they derived from the combination of a feeling of isolation and powerlessness within the group, into which he had been propelled, as well as from the attempt to resurrect a new basis of contacts and power among the group's participants.

It is perhaps helpful to see the situation in which Mr. Nahmani found himself after the discussion as confused and unclear. The management of the group had been wrested from him, and with it had been erased most of his ties and interest in the group. Moreover, no new medium for employing his organizational energy and interest had been forthcoming. Mr. Nahmani's exploratory stance in the new reality created for him, and his inclination not to stray from the former basis of his activity—the handicrafts group—was explained somewhat obliquely by him in his own words. In a conversation that I held with him, he referred to his new role in the group after its formalization. He suddenly recalled, ostensibly without reference to the present state of affairs, his work as a laborer in a large construction company from which he had retired early, following repeated quarrels with his bosses. He said: "I always held my ground, and didn't allow anyone to ride roughshod over me. I was ready to quit work rather than let others cramp my style; up to the time I did in fact leave I gave those who tried to trip me up plenty to think about." Although he did not address his remarks directly to what had occurred in the home, the mere fact of raising the matter of his position in the present institutional and group context, a position that had been largely determined by the kind of relationship he had with the manager, hints at the possibility that Mr. Nahmani himself drew

116

the analogy between past relations with his employers and his present problems with the manager.

Why did the confrontation between Mr. Nahmani and the manager take place? The reasons are varied, and in large measure personal factors are involved. It seems that in terms of the power structure of the home, the control exercised in occupying the residents, with its implications for the outside world, as well as within the home, is of central importance to manager and residents alike. The human actors who had had a part in the events leading to Mr. Nahmani's demise were the manager, Mr. Nahmani himself, members of the handicrafts group, as well of those of the discussion group—more specifically, the house committee. We shall now analyze the contribution of these individuals to the events described, and also to the relationships between them.

The source of Mr. Nahmani's power—his organizational and managerial skills in running the group—were dependent on the other residents who participated in the group. As noted, the group members themselves relied heavily on the manager, and mutual interests were apparent, especially with respect to holding the bazaar and making it a success. Mrs. Shimoni's group was not directly bound to Mr. Nahmani, as far as routine activities were concerned, and both types of loners could continue working without reference to him. In any case, it is clear that maintaining good relations with the manager was far more important to them than supporting Mr. Nahmani. Thus, when a confrontation crystallized between the manager and Mr. Nahmani, the latter was unable to enlist active support from among the participants, and in fact remained isolated in his struggle.

Why didn't Mr. Nahmani pursue extreme measures such as an open censure of the manager, leaving the home, etc.? There are several reasons for this, all connected with Mr. Nahmani's original situation when the crisis broke out. Mr. Nahmani was unable to bring into play outside pressures on the manager, but he could have left the home and managed well elsewhere, he maintained. (He claimed he would have received a tempting job offer if he had left the home). He did not do so because he was still involved in two groups in which he hoped to continue his activities, and perhaps even improve his standing.

Overt opposition to discussion of the handicrafts group in the discussion group would have endangered his position as secretary of the latter—a position he had not attained by virtue of outside connection or past activities. Virulent opposition to the holding of the discussion would not only have led to his banishment from the discussion group, but also brought about his total ejection from the handicrafts group. It should be remembered that Mr. Nahmani was not deprived of all activity, and nurtured ties with the instructress, indicating that he intended to establish a new stratum of relationships and apply his former strengths in certain directions. This is the typical pattern of crosscutting loyalties with other groups (see, for example, Gluckman 1960, 25).

What was the significance of involving the discussion group in the decision on Mr. Nahmani's future? If we view the matter from the manager's point of view, we will be able to appreciate the importance of the discussion group as an efficient tool for imposing his will on those residents outside of the group. His manipulation and exploitation of the group enables him to avoid direct and decisive confrontation with the resident, and to achieve his aims through the intervention of other residents, a ploy that prevents the resident from enlisting support within the home, especially since the members of the discussion group are influential. The establishment of the house committee responsible for the handicrafts group is crucial in this context, and taking it as a starting point, the function of the discussion group in the process described above is clear. The manager used it as a means to gain control of the occupational activity of residents in the home, based on his evaluation of the importance of such productive, handicraft work in the life of an old-age home. (At a later stage, group members charged that the manager of Mishan had, in fact, given them responsibility for all such occupational activity in the home.) The social composition of the members comprising the committee that manages the organizational and financial interests of the handicrafts group shows that as far as sources of power are concerned, they belong more to the social strata of the discussion group than to that of the handicrafts group. Facilitating the intervention of the discussion group did not derive solely from the manager's resolve, but from a shared interest with him in controlling the handicrafts group. The affair of the disciplinary court, which took place after Mr. Nahmani's death, shows that the cooperation worked well only up to a point. Then, when the house committee considered the time ripe to absorb certain additional institutional affairs into its own sphere of influence, it did not hesitate to try to do so, even in opposition to the manager's desires.

A comparison between the affair of the disciplinary court and the system of relations between Mr. Nahmani and the manager is instructive. While the factors occasioning Mr. Amit's decline were rooted in his relation with fellow members of the group, and not in the manager's greater power, the latter's success in removing Mr. Nahmani from the leadership of the handicrafts group was bound up with his influence over the activities of the handicrafts group—in other words, on the only source of Mr. Nahmani's power in the home. The affair can therefore be seen as part of the process of "adjustment" of the group to the manager's view of the home and its needs. For the members of the handicrafts group, the home was more "total" than for their counterparts in the discussion group. The former did not enjoy the abundance of choices available outside the home, did not nurture close ties with outside factors, and could not counter the use of the functioning weapon, should the manager choose to invoke it. In fact, this group constitutes an enabling framework for different groups of individuals with varied problems to organize their lives in the home by means of mutual cooperation. Mrs. Shimoni's circle, the nucleus of the group and its main "initiator of activity," insured itself against the risk of dismemberment, and acquired the potential of influencing the social structure of the home and stabilizing relationships within it. The loners who function found in the group a forum for demonstrating good functioning, while other loners used it as a means for reacting against different personal problems.

The group's foundation was not initiated by the manager, but its development and success brought about the creation of a new alignment of roles that ultimately were incorporated into the home and became a central feature of it. Although the manager's control of the group has increased, its very existence in the home was the result of the interplay of interrelations between the residents. This bears out the claim that the reality of the home must be structured not only against the background of relations between staff and residents, but also with due consideration given to the dynamic process of interrelationship amongst the residents themselves. The self-activity of residents changed the institutional structure, bringing in its wake a crystallization of new roles and creating new possibilities,

119

which were not proposed originally by the staff for the purpose of the organization of their lives within the home.

In this description of the relations between the manager and Mr. Nahmani, the dynamic aspect of the process of totality was stressed. This totality becomes more all-embracing for the same individual at different points in time. How is this increased intensity achieved? In the case being considered, totality did not emerge as a result of the direct contacts between manager and resident, but rather with the help of intervention by other residents—members of the discussion group. These individuals enjoy ties with the higher echelons of the formal organization to which the manager belongs, and "occupational therapy" is a subject in which these officials are interested[4] (e.g., the house committee's declaration that the director of Mishan himself asked this body to deal with occupational activities). In this way, a special structure for the imposition of "totality" on Mr. Nahmani was created. The manager "recruited" residents, whose ties with the formal organization were stronger than his own, in order to effect a resident's conformity with his purposes, which were also those of that same formal organization.

The handicrafts group is not only characterized by its influence on the change in structure of the home and the choices open to residents within it, but also by its incorporation into a new system created with almost exclusive reference to the reality within the home. It is in this light that it is possible to understand the view of the discussion group as an admired and almost sacred reference group. The spectrum of the references by members of Mrs. Shimoni's women's group toward the other residents ranged from the animals to the discussion group, and was confined to the boundaries of the home (in this respect, too, the home is a more total framework for them than for others). From this perspective, the standards adopted for self-evaluation and for the evaluation of others who participated in this group can be understood. The intellectual qualities ascribed to the discussion group and the absence of those qualities amongst the animals created for members of the handicrafts group the possibility of locating themselves in relation to other old people in the home. This also explains the seeming paradox evident when individuals engaged in physical activity adopt an intellectual yardstick.

The handicrafts group provided a framework in which, with the exception of Mr. Nahmani's case, there existed controlled cycles of repetition. Nor is there any linear progress. Each cycle of activity possesses a rhythm and order similar to those both preceding and following it. In Mr. Nahmani's case, this "law" was infringed upon in such a way that the cycle of the handicraft group's activities intruded into the manager's mobile career path.

The balance usually existing in the exchange relations between the manager and the women in the group constituted another dimension in the structuring of the possibility of change. The group allowed for varied and flexible maneuver in the demonstration of functioning, and even for a degree of individualism. As long as the basic rules of the game were not broken, the residents could feel secure from being ejected. They were also protected from a situation in which they were no longer able to construct a self-image of people able to create and to influence their world and their fate in it.

This feeling was enhanced as a result of the selective continuity existing in the kinds of activities pursued by the group. Most participants had been used to this kind of work in the past, so it did not create any potential catalyst for an identity crisis. Rather, it provided them with a feeling of existential continuity. In contrast to the case of the discussion group, there was no gap here between the world of content of the activity and the real power contained within it. From this standpoint, the mechanism used for the ordering of reality here was less problematic and more efficient.

121

6. THE SYNAGOGUE GROUP

Moberg and Taves (1965) cite a series of studies attesting to the importance of religious activity in adaptation to oldage (including the resident elderly in old age homes). According to their findings, the higher the level of participation in a religious framework, the more likely it is that the older person will be able to cope with the problem of old age confronting him. What then are the components of religious activity effecting this adjustment? Moves (1960) draws a distinction between the primary and secondary functions of religious activity among the elderly. Primary functions refer to general problems associated with old age and the imminence of death, illness, suffering, the feeling of nothingness, and so on. Secondary functions include status, social interaction, and the search for channels of social communication. If we take this approach as a starting point in the analysis of religious activity in the home, we find that for our purposes, the analysis of the secondary functions is more important sociologically.[1] We will pursue this point by clarifying the connection between the situation of the synagogue congregants in their "particular" institutional framework and their relationship to Jewish religious symbols, as seen against the background of their social "location." These symbols, of course, should not be seen solely as means through which residents cope with problems associated with residence in the home. They also provide essential foundations of meaning, impinging on the worshippers and actively influencing the exchange relationships between themselves, the staff, and other residents. At any event, the changes in the meaning of these symbols do not constitute deviations from the basic pattern of activity of the synagogue. This fact can be accounted for only by the importance of these particular symbols rather than others, as elements in the worldview of the worshippers.

There are two principal differences between the synagogue group and the two groups previously described: the motivation for membership amongst the worshippers is part of the customary pattern of their religious activity; it was not fashioned by the social reality within the home, but predated their entry into it.[2] It can be assumed that a good many of these individuals could not conceive of the possibility of leading orderly lives without the component of regular daily public prayer. None of the group began to participate in religious activity as a result of the social conditions prevailing in the home, nor did anyone "discover" religion in their old age. This qualitative difference between the synagogue group and the other groupings in the home raises a question, applicable only to the former group: How does residence in the home affect their pattern of religious activity? Since this activity derives, in part, from reference to specific religious symbols, it may be asked whether the fact of being residents in the home is discernable in these references amongst the group? This problem is tied to the central subject of our discussion, namely, the ways in which different groups of residents organize their lives in the home. Consequently, we must inquire, how does religious activity serve its followers in their ability to cope with the pressure arising from their institutionalization?

I

The general attitude toward religious activity in the home ranges from indifference to disrespect and scorn to outright hostility. Most of the residents do not regard themselves as religious, and some proclaim openly their opposition to and scorn of religion and the religious. It is possible that this attitude emanates from the fact that many of the more respected residents were in the past members of the socialist parties, which at certain periods reacted negatively to religion. But it also seems that a major reason stems from the character of the religious group itself, whose members are defined as operating on the very boundary of functioning. Most of the group are comparatively older than the nonobservant residents (their mean age being eighty-four), and this presupposes a declining state of health. Some of them experience increasing problems of mobility, having to use walking sticks, and in several cases, even the walls and other environmental supports to get around. Their condition prevents them from leaving their rooms very often, and when they do, it is to the synagogue, dining room, or toilets. A few try to avoid demonstrating their incapacities by utilizing rest periods to leave

124

their rooms. When walking, they do not look around, and generally choose the shortest route between their rooms and their destination. They are observed disdainfully by other residents, and even more so by the staff. In general,the attitude toward them approximates to that extended to the vegetables.

In addition to their characteristic, labored mobility, many of the group experience problems in maintaining any sort of social contact with the outside world. This is for two reasons: their mother tongue is Yiddish and some of them are not conversant with Hebrew at all. Despite the fact that most residents are fluent in it, Yiddish-speaking is considered, as was made clear earlier, second-rate, and it is preferable to abstain from its use. Furthermore, several synagogue congregants are incapable of piecing together an intelligible sentence. It is extremely difficult to induce them to speak, and even when they do, a stream of associations often result, whose meaning is totally unclear to the listener. They accept this as part of old age. In this respect, it can be said that their acknowledgement of the associated stigma is more marked than among other groups. Thus, for example, some of them admitted to "having something not quite right with me in the head" or proclaimed "I'm already old and se-nile." Sometimes the impression is gained that the self-ascription of the stigma helps them to rationalize to themselves and to others their nonparticipation in activities outside prayers. Goffman (1968, 21) notes this phenomenon of the use of stigma to explain away incapacity, or as an excuse for failure. In the synagogue context, it mainly operates when a demand is made on someone to intensify his participation, such as in the case of one congregant who was asked by his coworshippers to give them an extra lesson on the Talmud, in addition to their present quota (details of this will be given in due course). The man responded thus: "I can't do it, I'm weak, old, forget things and I don't see well—find someone else!"

The ties with the outside world prevailing among most of the religious group are too insubstantial to allow them to exert influence and power in order to lessen the risk of expulsion that hangs over them all. As was noted above, their social connections inside the home are also very limited, both because of their incapacity and, thus more cogently, because of the aversion aroused by them in the eyes of the other residents and the manager. If it is indeed true that this group operates on the borderline of good functioning and is in constant danger of deteriorating into a state of poor functioning, how does the synagogue serve as a bulwark for forestalling this risk? In order to answer this question, the way in which these individuals conduct their synagogue activity must be examined.

The synagogue was established on the initiative of several residents, headed by a prosperous South American who had settled in Israel in his senescence in order "to die in a holy place," as he put it. Since this man had enjoyed a central role among the Jewish community in his own country, had organized fund-raising for Israel, and had even personally contributed large sums, he was given a place in the home. He did not speak Hebrew, or have close ties with other residents—his considerable wealth being irrelevant to the overcoming of these problems—and was therefore consigned to spend half his day in the synagogue. He had also donated large sums of money to furnish and equip the place, and were it not for him, it is doubtful if a special area would have been set aside for religious activity. From its inception the task of organizing the synagogue was undertaken by Mr. Nahmani (the head of the handicrafts group and secretary of the discussion group). His involvement bestowed on the synagogue a form of "recognition" by other residents as a legitimate part of the home, worthy of respect. After he resigned from his role as synagogue secretary, two treasurers undertook this function, and were still doing so at the time of the research. One, a Mr. Mizrahi, of Tunisian extraction, was an "experienced," "qualified" treasurer, he claimed. He had established two synagogues in the course of his life, in communities where he had lived, and was very knowledgeable in managing a congregation. The second treasurer, a Mr. Goldstein, an Ashkenazi, could not claim such a background, but had succeeded in ingratiating himself with the congregants, and so was chosen.

The formal division of functions between the two was not at all clear. In fact, Mr. Mizrahi was responsible for collecting dues from the congregants, keeping accounts, purchasing equipment, and for various disbursements (to the cantor, the teachers, and the caretaker), but most importantly, for dealing with the manager. He claimed he submitted a balance sheet for the manager's approval every month, and such approval was publicized on the home's bulletin board. Mr. Mizrahi was one of the few residents who did remunerative work outside the home with the manager's knowledge and acquiescence. Mr. Goldstein, in contrast, was mainly preoccupied with "aliyot"—the allocation of roles among the congregation in the conduct of the religious service—so that Mr. Mizrahi called him, not without a hint of derision, "the treasurer of the aliyot." His ties with the other congregants were close, mainly because he could speak to them in Yiddish, understand their words, and respond appropriately. It should be noted, in this context, that most of the congregation, about twenty in number, were of Ashkenazi origin; one was a Yemenite, several were Bulgarians, and the rest were Sephardim of different extractions. In addition to the two treasurers, another member of the congregation served as a caretaker and received a payment of twenty lirot a month from synagogue funds, in exchange for preparing the room for prayer, for instruction in the Talmud, as well as tidying up after these activities. The rabbi was also one of the residents, and his role will be discussed in due course.

All of the congregants claim that some fifty people participate in prayer services every day. On the Shabbat, this rises to over a hundred, and on High Holidays "the whole home turns out." Actually, these estimates are gross exaggerations, for the daily attendance is only about fifteen, with the addition of a few outside visitors on Shabbatot, these usually being relatives of the congregants. On holidays, the synagogue is indeed full, but most of the additional worshippers are relatives of residents who visit the home on such occasions, as well as members of staff and their families. The situation regarding women is similar. Mr. Mizrahi, the treasurer, once claimed that "every woman in the home is Orthodox and all of them come to the woman's gallery." However, except for the Day of Atonement, the women's section is never full, and generally only about ten women are to be found. The incongruity existing between the claims of the congregation and reality derives from the desire of the former to view religious activity in the home as necessary and central. As such, it represents an attempt to improve the status of this activity in the home in the eyes of the manager by blurring the negative attitude towards it. This goal is also sought by relating it to the religious reality existing outside the home. Several worshippers claimed the status of religion in the country is improving, as more people are going to synagogue, and the number of the young attracted to religion is growing.

Typical of this view of external reality was a lively argument, conducted between two congregants, on the subject of which rabbi enjoyed higher stature in the realm of both learning and deeds,

127

Rabbi Lev or Rabbi Frankel. Each protagonist tried to prove his point by reference to the number of followers in the congregation of the rabbi he supported. Finally, the two agreed that both rabbis were very learned, and the important thing was, in the words of one of them, "that many people are now becoming religious and going to synagogue."

The use of this perception of the outside world for the purpose of reinforcing their status as religious people, both in their eyes and in the eyes of others, is not the only mechanism employed by religionists inside the home to enhance their position. The fact that this group straddles the very borders of functioning—in the sense that its members seem to be deteriorating in the eyes of the manager, both physically and mentally also determines the other avenues chosen by the group to demonstrate good functioning. They know that one of the main criteria for the demonstration of proper functioning is lively social involvement in the home. Consequently, they take considerable pains to create a suitable impression. They seek to achieve this aim not only by demonstrating their intensive investment in prayer, and inflating the number of congregants who participate, but principally they point to the variety of different groups flourishing under the synagogue's auspices.

II

In conversations with the congregants, many complained that the home expected them to show evidence of social activity. One of them expressed it this way: "Here in the home, the manager wants us to be busy all the time, but we don't want to bombard him with all kinds of suggestions, like the rest of them. Whoever goes to synagogue does not go to the movies or to plays." Here we have an excuse for the lack of participation by the religious group in other activities in the home, which is rooted in their system of religious concepts and values. "We are not libertines," and similar excuses were forthcoming from other group members, such as: "We don't attend Bible class because it's not difficult enough, it's not serious, it's for women." What then, if this is true, is the substitute found by the synagogue group for these activities?

The group held four hour-long lessons every week, two in Talmud and two in Aggada (legend). The lessons in the Talmud are given by a rabbi specially hired for this purpose by the congregants, while Aggada instruction is in the hands of a volunteer from outside the home. What happens in these lessons? The group is fastidious about promptness. In front of every "student" the relevant book has been set out, in advance, by the steward. The teacher reads and interprets in Yiddish, despite the fact that some "students" do not understand the language. No questions are asked, and if remarks are made, these are usually digressions. Some participants do not even turn the pages, and many adopt an unchanging sitting posture throughout. Some whisper between themselves, being periodically interrupted by a reproof from Mr. Mizrahi. In contrast, Mr. Goldstein sits silently throughout, uninvolved in either the lesson or conversations. At any event, he does not venture any comment to those around him. Mr. Mizrahi hums oriental melodies quietly to himself and glances at his watch every now and then, in order to see if the time has come for the lesson to end. He also does not turn over any pages—sometimes reading aloud a line or two, irrespective of what the teacher is saying.

The teacher, who is unable to evoke any reactions, manages in this fashion to struggle through about a page and a half of Talmud per lesson, so that the "students" can pride themselves that they are progressing apace with their studies. According to almost any criteria, this may be considered a very fast pace for Talmudic learning, which is uncharacteristic even of outstanding rabbinic scholars. Thus, it attests only to the thoroughly superficial nature of this study enterprise. It is absolutely clear that the participants do not comprehend the content of the lessons. Testimony to this fact can be found in the words of the rabbi, who said of them that "they are worse than ignoramuses, and don't even understand the meaning of the words in the prayerbook." Nevertheless, many of the congregants wanted the treasurers to organize more lessons on weekdays as well as the Shabbat, because "what we have now is not sufficient." One of the participants, perhaps the only one in fact besides the rabbi, who knows some Talmud, was asked by his fellows to teach an additional page daily. To this he replied: "I'm already old and don't remember my studies. But apart from that we have a genius of a rabbi here, and how can I compete with him?" It seems likely that in this instance the man's argument was not an excuse because he is the only member of the congregation whom the rabbi values as a scholar. Both he and the rabbi occasionally study Tal-

129

mud outside the framework of the lessons, while the others in the synagogue make no effort to even turn the pages of their prayer books.

What then is the significance of this framework of study? Clearly, the congregants are unable to relate to the subject matter— but this notwithstanding, they continue to participate and even seek to expand it. The need to demonstrate good functioning, and the absence of other areas of activity for such demonstration in the home for them, are apparently the key factors sustaining the existence of the study framework. The knowledge that the management looks upon officially sanctioned group activity favorably, spurs the group to persist with the lessons as confirmation of their functioning. Most of those attending the lessons had never engaged in a similar activity prior to their entry into the home. This fact supports our assumption that living in an institution, with its special conditions, helped shape this activity. We have here a pattern of accepted religious activity (Talmudic studies) bereft almost entirely of its original subject matter, which is purported to be pure study. The external framework of the religious symbol remains, whereas the sphere of meaning that colors the symbol is determined by the non-religious (and perhaps even the antireligious) reality that surrounds the referents to it.[3] In effect, the framework of the symbol has become the main subject of its content.

Support for this view of the instructional activity in the synagogue is forthcoming from the analysis of one aspect of the congregant's behavior that bears directly both to their place in the home and their efforts to improve it. The congregants pay a monthly subscription of five lirot. In addition, donations are obtained from residents who request memorial prayers for their deceased, or who participate in the reading of the Law of the Torah (Aliyot), from visitors, and from the allocation of seats on holidays. The overall monthly income is about two hundred lirot. Expenses comprise payment to the cantor, to the teacher, refreshments for the congregants on Shabbat, the purchase of religious books, and running expenses, so that at the end of the month there is usually no surplus. Despite this, the treasurers, with the consent of the congregation, budgeted for a donation of three hundred fifty lirot to the Soldiers' Welfare Committee. From the earlier description of the handicrafts group's activities, it will be remembered how important the work for this committee was deemed to be in the home, and how esteemed were those who took part in it. This has not escaped the attention of the congregants, and they sought to be considered amongst those working on behalf of the committee by giving a donation. Here also, as in the study activity, there is adherence to external signs of good functioning, without any attempt at substantiating them with any content. The importance of activity on behalf of the Soldiers' Welfare Committee is essentially to be found in the occupation it entails and not actually in the donation of funds.

III

The legitimation of synagogue activity for a purpose defined as not necessarily religious, and the characteristics of the congregants who sustain this activity, are brought into relief by the personality of the rabbi of the synagogue and his attitude toward his congregation. The rabbi is a sickly man of eighty-seven, who says of himself that "I don't remember any more, or hear well, and feel very weak." His Hebrew is fluent and he is the only one (except for those congregants of Oriental origin) who does not converse with his fellows in Yiddish. Before he entered the home, he had published several religious books, had run a key department of the Religious Affairs Ministry, and claimed close ties with some famous rabbinical figures, including the Chief Rabbi Herzog ("who loved him like his own soul") and the Chief Rabbi Uziel ("whom we greatly respected"). According to himself and those who knew him, he was considered "a diligent scholar," "perceptive and knowledgeable," "a great rabbi," "very learned," and other similar epithets.

Nevertheless, despite his respected status as a rabbi and excellent relations with the religious establishment, he took pains to emphasize two other aspects of his life: his former status as a "prisoner of Zion" in the USSR, and his acquisition of a certificate from the Histadrut in recognition of his work on their behalf. He keeps this certificate permanently in his pocket. From time to time, he habitually asks whoever he is engaged in conversation with whether they have already seen it, and without waiting for an answer, takes the document from its protective envelope, unfolds it, and urges his companion to read it carefully. Similarly, the rabbi contributes occasionally to the home's newspaper, always writing on nationalistic subjects, such as: "Diaspora and Redemption," "The Independence of

131

Israel," "The Prophetess Deborah as a National Leader," and so on. To what does all this attest? The rabbi's good relations with religious dignitaries outside the home cannot help him cope with the problems posed by his residence in the home. Here the question of his good functioning is not specifically at issue. (Although, since he is not a healthy man, but moves around with some difficulty, this factor should not be overlooked.) Rather, it expresses the way he sees himself in an institutional framework that does not particularly value religious activity, and to which the more respected residents do not ascribe any value.

The rabbi seems to adopt some of the standards of evaluation obtaining within the home. The emphasis on the nonreligious aspects of his personality and life shows that he is striving to characterize himself in the eyes of others, and possibly in his own eyes, in terms of those traits common to members of the discussion group. All three points already suggested support this claim. First, his status as a Prisoner of Zion—activity and self-sacrifice on behalf of Zionism. Second, his certificate from the Histadrut—the selfsame ties with the outside world, which he enjoys together with most of the discussion group members. Third, his newspaper articles—his attachment to members of the group who also contribute (indeed, they are practically the only individuals who do so). The assumption of these institutional yardsticks for evaluation is reflected also in the rabbi's attitude toward his congregants.

In his view, the home's synagogue is not imbued with any unique or special character, being rather "a big jumble of different approaches to religion, different prayers, communities and leaders—the congregants have nothing in common by way of uniformity or knowledge." As the rabbi uttered these remarks, he did not hesitate to point with disdain to those congregants sitting in front of him. His personal conclusion, which he had reached, so he claimed, as a result of living amid such individuals, was: "I don't have anyone to talk to, certainly not on religious matters. I don't feel at home here." The rabbi does not even converse with the congregants, with the exception of one individual ("a wise and learned scholar"), rarely attends Talmud classes, and when he does so, it is only for a few minutes, "just because the teacher is a personal friend." He is clear about the quality of the lessons: "The teacher instructs well, and his explanations are good. But all his words fall on deaf ears. They don't understand anything. It's a waste of time." For him, the reason for the continued existence of the lessons is "to be together, that's what they want and not to study at all." The rabbi does not explain the meaning of this "togetherness," for in fact the social contacts within the congregation are so limited that most of the participants do not even know the names of their fellow worshippers, with whom they pray daily. It seems the interplay of two kinds of tension cause the rabbi to hold such a negative view of the congregants. First, there is a vast gulf between his level of religious knowledge, education, and mode of religious activity, as compared with that of the other congregants. Second, there is a sense of social distance resulting from his self-evaluation, as belonging to the home's activists, and his awareness of the status of the congregants in the institution. The rabbi is unable to skip public prayer, and because of his physical condition he cannot attend an outside synagogue, so that he is forced to come into regular close daily contact with the congregants. It can be assumed this exacerbates his sense of alienation, between them and himself, reinforcing his negative attitude towards his fellow religionists.

It appears that since the rabbi has more in common with members of the discussion group than with his own congregation, he inflates the degree of totality of the institution experienced by his coreligionists in the synagogue, as expressed in his attitude toward them. Their dependence on the home is so pronounced that it brings about changes in the nature of the religious symbols to which they refer. The necessity for group activity stems from the marginal place of the synagogue in the eyes of the management and of other residents. But what happens when due to special circumstances the synagogue occupies "center stage" in the institutional life of the home? Does the behavior of the congregants change in concert? Do they feel a reduction in the totality of the home towards them? In the following sections we will try to describe the changes that took place in the synagogue during the High Holidays.

IV

On the Jewish New Year, and even more so on the Day of Atonement, the synagogue was packed with worshippers, some in the synagogue itself, others in the corridor leading to it. Many worshippers were not residents, but staff members and relatives who were visiting

133

during the holiday period. Four events that occurred during this period are pertinent to the issue of the organization of institutional life and our understanding of totality within it. The first two episodes relate to the tension between the resident population in the synagogue and the manager, whereas the latter two teach us something more about the attitude of the manager, the congregation, outside visitors, and the staff toward the vegetables.

The treasurer, Mr. Mizrahi, was not present at any of the prayer services because he spent the holiday period with his family. There he prayed in his local synagogue, which he had used prior to his entry into the home, and in which he had even served as treasurer. This presented a golden opportunity for Mr. Goldstein, the other treasurer, to act without fear of being upstaged by Mr. Mizrahi. He positioned himself next to the cantor and his assistants. After the evening service for the New Year had been completed, and the congregation was ready to disperse, he mounted the platform, silenced those present, and announced: "Anyone who did not buy a seat for the High Holidays shouldn't come tomorrow. I repeat—whoever didn't pay should go home and not return any more. I can see here a lot of people who didn't buy a seat and I am warning them not to come here again." The congregation listened in shocked silence and then began to disperse, many of them uttering resentful comments such as: "What nerve—it isn't his synagogue!" "I can pray anywhere I like," or "I came because I pay enough to keep my father here, and I'm not going to pay anymore!" and so on. The manager was not present at the time and this has to be taken into account in understanding the impact of Mr. Goldstein's outburst. The treasurer was in fact directing his remarks to the regular congregation, rather than to the uninvited guests. His object was to demonstrate to them that he was in charge now, in the absence of Mr. Mizrahi, of the handling of relations with outsiders and that he was looking after their interests. It seems likely that this incident is a function of the ongoing rivalry between Mr. Goldstein and Mr. Mizrahi for influence over the congregants and the running of the synagogue. Until this opportunity arose, Mr. Mizrahi's close ties with the manager had prevented Mr. Goldstein from developing as a leader with influence over his fellow congregants, and his functions were generally restricted to organizing the study activities and keeping order during lessons.

The absence of both Mr. Mizrahi and the manager created a

temporary situation where there was no one "in charge of" the congregants, and this vacuum was exploited by Mr. Goldstein. In the course of his demonstration of power (directed at the regular population of worshippers), Mr. Goldstein offended, albeit unintentionally, many of the home's visitors. These visitors are very important to the manager for a variety of reasons. Therefore, offending them is akin to demonstrating opposition to the manager himself. The manager's principal source of power is derived from outside sources (see chapter 3). Consequently, he makes a great effort to create a positive image for the home in the eyes of visitors (see chapter 5). How important the visitors are to the manager, and how far the influence of his presence extends over the congregants, will be shown in the following event.

On the eve of the Day of Atonement, many visitors who had been unable to secure for themselves places in the synagogue gathered near its entrance, filling the corridor. For some reason, the light in the corridor had not been switched on earlier. Of course no one dared to do this on the eve of the holiday, since it was now past the time and forbidden by Jewish law. During the *Kol Nidre* prayers many visitors had opened their prayer books, but had found it hard to read because of the darkness. The manager, who was inside the synagogue and standing in the center of the first row, saw what was happening outside. He left his place, hurried to the corridor, and switched on the light. He then returned to his seat. Some of the congregation were so shocked by this that they ceased praying, but no one actually said anything, and apart from some indistinct mutterings amongst the ranks of the visitors, no reaction was forthcoming. Prayers continued unaffected. Despite this blatant infringement of a central religious symbol, the congregants did not react at all (at least openly). Nor did their reticence derive from their characteristic passivity, for on the same day some minutes after this incident, one of the female residents entered the men's section of the synagogue by mistake. Several of the worshippers left their places, rebuked her loudly, and physically pushed her out into the corridor. If we add to this the "honors" bestowed on the manager during the High Holidays, such as the opening of the Ark, we can appreciate the extent of the influence of the man on this group, which in his estimation hovers on the borderline of functioning. This is yet another aspect of the all-embracing totality emcompassing those individuals. In this case, it may be seen by the intrusion of the manager

135

into their religious life, through the desecration of a central symbol—an act that did not elicit any reaction.

V

The High Holidays brought into the precincts of the synagogue people with diverse backgrounds. Since it is a small place, and many people were trying to crowd in, there were numerous cases of friction. Despite this congestion, no quarrels erupted among those present. The only exception involved the presence of the "vegetables" in the synagogue. Several of these individuals, who show no interest in any activity outside eating and going to and from their rooms, appeared near the synagogue on the eve of the Day of Atonement and at its close. Two incidents will further our understanding of what happened, in the context of their appearance.

First, however, in order to understand these incidents, a detailed description of the location of the synagogue is required. It is situated inside the building, with its windows facing the lawn surrounding the home, with two of its doorways facing the corridor of the lower floor. The first doorway is situated at the front of the synagogue. Opposite it, an elevator has been installed so that the space between the doorway and the elevator is very narrow, but conversely, very negotiable for anyone who has difficulty getting around. The other doorway is situated at the back of the synagogue, near the women's section. The distance to be transversed from the elevator to this doorway is many times greater than that from the elevator to the first doorway. Between the elevator door and the first doorway a large crowd blocking the entrance to the synagogue had assembled.

After the *Kol Nidre* service, the elevator door opened to reveal one of the residents recognized as a vegetable. He is a hunchback, who has considerable difficulty in moving around, and he utilizes both a cane and the walls to support himself while he walks. The elderly people standing beside the elevator made no effort to enable the man to exit the elevator. Only the rebukes of some of the visitors persuaded them to make way for him, and allow the man to leave the elevator. When the door closed behind him, he tried to make a path for himself through the crowd. But the surrounding residents turned a blind eye. One of the visitors appealed to them: "Why don't

136

you help him?" This plea, too, went unheeded—save for one elderly man who said somewhat apologetically: "Well then, what can be done, this is an old-age home, and this is what one expects to find in it."[4] One female visitor tried to grasp his hand and lead him to the doorway opposite the elevator. However, the man eluded her, and remarked "over there is nearer"—directing his steps toward the far doorway. (It should be recalled that the manager had stationed himself opposite the elevator inside the synagogue, and this may provide the explanation for the old man's behavior.) When he reached his destination, following a slow and tortuous progress, none of the home's residents vacated a seat for him. It was left to a visitor to find a chair and offer it to him. Did the old man go to the far entrance, because he was wary of meeting the manager? A partial answer to this can perhaps be found in the following incident.

During the concluding prayers on the Day of Atonement, the elevator door opened, revealing a female resident with a walking aid (same device as will be recalled having aroused reservations on the part of both the manager and residents), waiting to get out. Several other female residents, who had been blocking the exit, did not allow her to advance, and she tried to push them out of her way. A number of female visitors told the residents that they should make way for the woman, but this did not elicit any response.

Another resident in the "vegetable" category happened on the scene and one of those blocking the way called out: "Shove her into the elevator as well," to which her friends responded by collectively pushing the unsuspecting resident toward the elevator, pushing her inside the doors closing on the two unfortunates, and the elevator ascending.

After a moment the elevator returned, and as the door opened it revealed the elderly lady with the walker. This time one of the service workers saw what was happening, held the door open, and assisted the old lady to emerge while clearing a path for her. This operation took some time. Finally, the manager, who had been in the synagogue during the incident, realized that confusion reigned outside, and came over to investigate what was happening. When he saw the worker trying to "rescue" the old lady from the elevator he rebuked him for allowing the elevator to stand idle for such a long time, threatened to put it out of service completely, and ordered the employee to allow the doors to close. The man obeyed and the door closed. Shortly afterwards, the elevator arrived yet again, the doors opened, and the old lady reappeared. By this time the housemother had arrived on the scene and asked the old lady what she wanted. She replied that she had come to hear the blowing of the lamb's horn, *Shofar*. Saved at last, the housemother assisted her to emerge from the elevator and led her to the women's section.

In both incidents, one finds in the residents' behavior toward their handicapped fellows a form of denial of the phenomenon of disability, through the medium of exaggerated avoidance and rejection. Even when force of circumstances involves close, even physical, contact, the "healthy" residents are not prepared to acknowledge the presence or the basic human rights of the handicapped. It is conceivable that the very presence of the visitors exacerbated this avoidance behavior. In relating to the handicapped differently, the visitors were bestowing a kind of recognition on them, being in the last analysis part of the home and worthy of the same rights as the other residents. It seems that the barrier erected by the residents toward the handicapped (mental or physical—there is no possibility of making a finer distinction) cannot be broken down, even when both parties find themselves in a direct confrontation. This was most striking in the case of the synagogue congregants toward the man in the first example. Some of these individuals were themselves approaching the same life situation, and perhaps because of this, their desire to preserve the barrier between themselves and the man was stronger than that of other residents.

The ability of the synagogue group to maneuver within the home with the help of their outside connections (like the discussion group) or through internal activity (like the handicrafts group) is extremely limited. Moreover, their state of health renders them on the borderline of good functioning. The measure of dependence of this group is the greatest of the three groups discussed. It shows itself in an almost absolute acceptance of the validity of the institutional standards for evaluating residents. This, in turn, involves the adaptation of learning and Jewish study as a religious symbol, to what for them appears to be a criterion for evaluation within the institution (group activity). This adjustment is so deep-seated that they cannot allow themselves to react to an infringement of another religious symbol by the manager. The institutional framework shapes the form and content of the religious symbol. The marginality of the synagogue within the home (in regard to the type of participant and the attitude toward religious activity generally)

138

does not allow it to function as a pivotal force in influencing what transpires there (as opposed to the status of the handicraft group, for example). Even on the rare occasions when it becomes the center of interest in the home (during the High Holidays), its influence is temporary and lacks significance in terms of the prevailing attitude towards the worshippers and their activities. Nor did it prevent the manager, who was more concerned with his visitors, from offending one of their main religious symbols.

The physical difficulties of the congregants, coupled with their tacit acceptance of the stigma of senility and the intellectual frailty wrought by aging, preclude them from creating a distinction on a physical or mental basis between them and other old people. The only factor distinguishing them is connected to their activity in a group framework, which does not obtain amongst the vegetables. This distinction also is manifest in their acceptance of the evaluative criteria framed by the home, their collusion with labelling imposed on them by others. The attitude of the group of worshippers towards other handicapped residents stemmed from, among other things, their isolation and lack of any group framework, which might enable them to enjoy a more positive relationship with the management (in terms of their demonstration of functioning).

The most striking characteristic of the dependence emerging from the description of the synagogue is that connected with the extent of the penetration of the manager's influence on the residents' lives. No verifiable or exact measure of the influence is available, but it seems that the changes that occurred in a central religious symbol resulted from the reality of the home, the depth of reaction to the harm done to another symbol, and the almost complete acceptance of evaluative criteria developed within the home— all these things point to the all-embracing nature of the institution's influence over the lives of the synagogue group.

Here also, as with the handicraft group, we find a cyclical framework of activity bereft of any element of mobility or progress. Here too, there exists selective continuity of a pattern of behavior from the past, adapted to the structuring of a reality devoid of change in the present. Although space for maneuver regarding functioning is smaller in this case, it nevertheless still serves as the primary instrument in the framing of a picture of the world in which the home occupies center-stage, and the desire to remain in it without vulnerability to the dangers posed by the outside world. This is an organizing principle strong enough to introduce a new existential order, which facilitates a categorical division between old people, determining criteria for self-evaluation, and even capable of leading to far-reaching manipulations of patterns of faith and tradition.

7. CONCLUSION: MANAGING CHANGE — A SYNCHRONIC PERSPECTIVE

The dynamic, turbulent character of social life in the home seems a far cry from the image of the aged suffering from the degenerating, institutionalization syndrome so commonly portrayed in the sociological literature.[1] Moreover, the vitality of the residents is not commensurate with the passivity and withdrawal generally associated with the elderly. Yet paradoxically, the tremendous amount of energy expended that charges the activities described is directed toward the preservation and the retention of the immutable. In other words, the state of unchangeability sought is best achieved and maintained by a continuous, dynamic social process. Thus, the task of resisting change requires just as much ingenuity, determination, and resourcefulness as would be expected from the opposite, that is, engendering change. What qualified the home in question to serve as an arena for such an enterprise? What are the structural properties of its institutional activity, that invested it with this paradoxical potential for its residents?

I

Unlike certain segregated institutional settings, or even noninstitutional retirement communities,[2] our home is an inseparable part of a much broader sociocultural milieu. Hence the pressures, as well as the stimulation experienced by inmates, are anchored in an external set of factors. Furthermore, the bureaucratic setup in the home intensifies and exacerbates such dilemmas, to the extent that the universal existential problem of confronting impending change in later life is magnified and inescapable. Residents are left with no alternative but to respond to the power structure prevailing in the institution, and thus involve themselves, willingly or otherwise, in a web of relationships that can be subsumed and analyzed as regularization mechanisms, to use Moore's (1975) term.

In the following discussion we will attempt to evaluate the properties of this change-coping device, in relation to its function in the proposed introductory model. Clearly the experience of change is embedded as a fundamental existential problem in the life of the aged (see the Introduction). Thus, the reconstruction processes in each of the three groups may be viewed as a response to this universal characteristic of the later years. In this respect, it cuts across sociocultural and economic boundaries dividing individuals and groups of various backgrounds operating under very different cultural circumstances.

The management of change, as manifested in the behavior of the members of each of the three groups consistently exemplifies several common unitary elements that together form a patterned strategy mode of change-resistance.

A brief review of the facets of this mechanism include the following:

1) The adoption of a nonfuturistic time perspective. Specifically, the residents do not engage in long-term planning and mobility-oriented projects. Any accumulation of institutional "credits" or resources is designed solely to enhance prospects of avoiding prospective changes. No linear, progressively designed pursuit of goals beyond that destination can be detected in the residents' behavior.

2) Alongside this control and neutralization of the future a sense of continuity with the past is maintained. The prevalent symbolic codes are rooted in the life histories and cultural background of the residents. Thus resisting change does not necessarily entail a disengagement from previous experiences. Retrospective references are designed to sustain and solidify present identities by reconstructing life reviews that are institutionally conditioned and shaped.

3) The institutional-based worldview of categorization and cognitive boundaries internalized by the residents are static and rigid. Any hint of transmutation of elements between categories is rendered unacceptable.

4) The organization of reality in this context is coherent, embracing almost any situation or interaction. Hence the total-

142

ity of this change-proof orientation is thoroughly divorced from, and sometimes contrary to, the totality of the institution as a bureaucratically bound power structure.

Notwithstanding the general properties of the change-resistance mechanism, it is important to stress that each group and individual member developed their own versions of that mechanism. These divergent variations, although signifying the uniqueness of each group, do not deviate from the above fundamental pattern. Surveying the variegated forms of handling change in each of the three groups provides an insight into the means by which specific conditions are molded in the adaptations to a commonly shared existential dilemma.

First, it is important to begin by observing that the three groups differ broadly in their respective modes of negotiation and bargaining positions. Clearly, the degree of dependency among members of the discussion group on the staff is far less than that of the synagogue regulars. In both groups an imbalance in the relationships exists, enabling one party to possess and wield more power than its counterparty. The craft group, however, seems to have been engaged in a fairly balanced reciprocity, based on a power structure where negotiated order was governed by mutual interests and common goals.

It should also be noted that these differences among the three groups are anchored in nonsimilar sets of relationships. The activities of the discussion group were shaped mainly by the interaction among the members and by their associations with the non-institutional environment. The members of the synagogue, however, generally acted as separate individuals vis-à-vis the manager, whereas the participants in the craft group presented a more cohesive front.

These differences are, to a large extent, projections of affiliations with the outside world that circumscribe each group, with their own set of sociocultural boundaries. If the delineation of these boundaries is determined by the perceived range of viable existential alternatives open to residents, then the members of the discussion group seemed to enjoy a broad spectrum of options. The craft group was relatively restricted, and hence its scope of choices was confined to various manipulations in constructing institutional life. Finally, the members of the synagogue were not only compelled by

143

the setting, but also experienced a very narrow leeway of plausible courses of action, within which maneuvering could be made constructive.

Evidently, these boundaries are also reflected in the residents' views concerning the home's internal social stratification system. In this respect, there was a highly reified conception of relative grading and esteem attached to social positions in the institution. The self-glorified members of the discussion group were unanimously regarded as the haloed and hallowed institutional elite. Conversely, only a thin line separated the members of the synagogue from the dehumanized category of vegetables and animals. Yet, the different measures taken by the groups to safeguard their respective stations all shared one common denominator, interwoven with their attempts to forestall adverse change—there was no apparent desire to vie for a higher status. This should therefore be considered as another constituent in the social reinforcement of immobility, and hence, in the mechanism of resisting change.

Although members of the groups shared the same set of values for social esteem, they diverged in their criteria for evaluating suitability to the home. Each acknowledged differently a resident's capacity and right to remain unremoved. The discussion group, having adopted a physiological-functional measure, adhered to a division quite opposite to the intellectually based differentiation fostered by members of the craft group. In the case of the synagogue, however, neither physical nor mental criteria were applied; instead, identification with, and commitment to, association with a group activity in and of itself was taken to be a badge of a resident's competence to survive in the institution.

The symbolic code implicit in the process of categorization in the home relates to three degrees of autonomy of realms of meaning. The residents' values, beliefs, and modes of behavior are differentially affected by institutional life. The organizational characteristics of the home differentially pervade these three respective symbolic orders, as manifested in the groups' conduct.

Thus, declarations about the central significance of personal action made by members of the discussion group remained unchanged compared to attitudes in their preinstitutional life. They not only maintained this position, but reinforced and reiterated it at a higher and almost unrestrained level. The institutional setting, given its power structure, provided the necessary prerequisites for members of the group to invest old symbols with newly modified meanings, to serve as tools for reconstructing their social identity. The symbolic world of the participants of the craft group was only slightly altered, to function as a resource within the institutional setup. The deepest and most significant penetration of the context of the home into the existential experience of residents occurred in the lives of the members of the synagogue, where major transformations of meaning were introduced as strategies for survival in the institution. The three cases demonstrate a range of plausible balances between spheres of relevance and fields of control.

II

It is clear that spheres of relevance and fields of control are not mutually exclusive existential dimensions, but rather analytic devices serving to elucidate aspects of constructing reality. The substantive descriptions presented in this book are designed to illustrate these two sets of rules with ethnographic material, which, in itself, might be interpreted in either way.[3]

The third element of the model, change, is also not seen as a given quality of social life, but rather a negotiable property of action and interaction. Unlike most perspectives on life changes that advocate the conception of a transition through stages,[4] roles[5] and identities, *our approach regards change itself as a socially constructed reification of prospective uncertainties.* This view strips the notion of transformation of its "objective" connotations. Such a perspective seems closely related to ethnomethodological arguments concerning the nature of social life, particularly to themes developed by Gubrium and Buckholdt (1977), who maintain that the very concept of maturity as a form of perceived life-change is a product of ongoing negotiation between members of social situations. Notwithstanding the similarity, it should be stressed that our model postulates the experience of impending uncertainty—change—as an ominous possibility, impinging heavily on the procedures and content of constructing reality and thus rendering it "real."

If terms such as "organization of activities," "procedures," "rules," or "methodology" are deemed conceptually meaningful and thus sociologically explicable, it is imperative to preconceive of the need for order among humans as an essential, without which the

145

fundamentals of phenomenology itself could be proven to be invalid. Hence, the need to structure uncertainty[6] is treated here as the only axiomatic[7] behavioral principle underlying our analysis. Change, therefore, is transmuted into a basic existential precondition, or a guiding rule, without which an understanding of self-conception vis-à-vis retrospective and prospective behavior cannot be complete. This premise leads to a consideration of the temporal properties of the model.

It is almost taken for granted in the relevant literature that any paradigm of adjustment—not necessarily pertaining to old age—should follow a diachronic-linear direction along which themes of continuity, transition, passage and progression are reflected and sustained. Much of the recent literature on the anthropology of aging has centered mainly around two foci of analysis. There are studies of structural changes in social boundaries,[8] alongside a growing corpus of research on the reconstruction of life histories, as a manifestation of the alleged ubiquitous desire for a sense of continuity in ordering the experience of one's life.[9] Both trends lean on the assumption that the reconstruction of reality among the aged is an emergent property of past experience and retrospective considerations. Neither trend, however, regards the plausibility of a synchronic analytic mechanism as a viable approach to problems of change. This by no means represents the proposal of a radical theoretical alternative that discounts existing approaches to the study of old age. Rather, it shifts the emphasis from etic and emic premises concerning the chronological sequential nature of temporal experience to a perspective that views social dynamics as a product of situationally anchored structures of balance between relevance and control.

Ironically, outside of the field of social gerontology there is little real novelty in this approach, with its theoretical foundations grounded in a long tradition of sociological thought. The Simmelian[10] idea that preceded Bateson's[11] analysis of the nature of play and the double bind, Goffman's "frames"[12], and Turner's insights into the prominence of the antistructure of communitas[13] are just a few representations of the notion of atemporal perspectives on social life. In all of these instances, however, still-time[14] is merely an analytic device to capture certain properties of social action. Our material here takes us far beyond the limits of such an objective, to viewing the arrest of unpredictable sequential time—change—as an existential strategy of survival. Deciphering the rules of this mechanism will allow for the postulation of a continuum along which diverse forms of change-management modes can be ordered. The ultimate end of atemporality is a state created by an absolute control of relevance either through reconstruction of meaning to tailor a contextually bound set of negotiating procedures, or through enhancing perceived manipulability in accordance with worlds of significance. When such a balance is achieved, the sequential dynamics generating diachronic, planning-laden time orientations are converted into a reflexive[15] self-transformatory power. Such conditions are typical of a host of social situations which, although not directly related to aging, nevertheless evince similar structural properties to those described in a number of studies of the social world of the aged.[16] These are autotelic systems such as play,[17] dance,[18] "good times",[19] the liminal stage in rites of passage,[20] and probably certain mental conditions diagnosed as mental illness. The other end of the continuum represents teleological situations where ends and means are discrepant. Here we are dealing with a prospective, future-oriented dynamic of a regularized set of activities directed at desired spheres of relevance. Such social phenomena are instilled with controllable, predictable change, enabling the actor to conceive of his future as sustained by, and contained within, the situational boundaries of his present.[21]

Traditional models of adjustment to old age explicitly or implicitly regard the aging process as a sequence of responses to changing physical, environmental, and sociocultural conditions. Although certain recent theories emphasize the active part taken by the aged person in determining and constructing his own reality, the presumption often still remains that the relationship between social context and the individual operating within it is the paramount axis for understanding adaptation. While not discounting this approach, our proposed model suggests a shift in foci of observation and analysis, from the content of contextual impact to its organization and structuring by the individual.

Expressions of this perspective can be found through reexamination of other ethnographic material on aging, especially studies concerning the symbolic manifestations of continuity in cultural identity. One of the most notable examples in that line is Myerhoff's study of the social world of elderly Jews in a day center in Venice, California (Myerhoff 1979). A revitalization of what seemed to the

147

members as their indigenous tradition, embedded in the culture of the East European shtetel, constituted the core of their collective self-esteem, social bonds, and sense of existential continuity. Group activities, ceremonies, social relationships, and artistic preoccupations were all impregnated with meanings of interconnectedness with the perceived past and the envisioned mythical future of the Jewish people. Structurally, a nonlinear, mythical time conception overrode the ordinary chronological perspective; identification with their Jewish heritage and fate was rendered plausible and controllable. The cyclical dimension of their symbolic code took precedence over the linearly dominated extra-center milieu. Thus, selection of means of expression reflects the members' existential universe both in content and in structure.[22] Continuity, therefore, can be treated not merely as a guiding principle for constructing one's universe; it is also a significant dimension of the spheres of relevance, which together with fields of control, dialectically constitute the life world of the individual aged.

None of the groups in the home can be fitted perfectly into the model. It is too schematic, too ideal, and too neat to genuinely encapsulate any given behavior. Indeed, reflection or typological description do not constitute the purpose or the intent in the conceptualization of the model. Instead, it is intended to serve as an analytic device, based on a fundamental set of propositions, that provides an alternative perspective on issues of importance in the field of aging. It is what Schneider has called "a model of defined parts" (Schneider 1965), and as such its relation to any observable reality is primarily heuristic. Thus, the groups in the home represent modes of striving for, and being drawn into, situations structurally akin to the hypothetical state proposed by the model.

III

Returning to the original subject of the explanatory relevance of the model to the case of the elderly, it can be argued that its propositions suggest an escape from the long-standing and sterile debate concerning the intricacy of the relationship between imputed universal patterns of aging and specific, culturally conditioned modes of growing old. From Simmons's (1945) theory of universal needs, its elaboration by Cowgill and Holmes (1972), and on to Cumming and Henry (1961), whose universal disengagement theory presented a challenge to cultural relativism,[23] to Guttman's (1964, 1969) psychoanalytic perspective, to life stages approaches,[24] and Myerhoff and Simic's (1978) conviction in the generic nature of the struggle for continuity in the self-construction of life histories—all are landmarks of the quest for universality underlying the aging process. Notwithstanding the diversity of these research agendas, and the very different sets of premises upon which they are based, it is evident that the search for a behavioral common denominator, as an analytic key to the understanding of old people, is characteristic to them all. Our approach, however, considers behavior, attitudes, psychological variables, and social constraints to be of secondary importance to the relationships between them.

Thus, following Henry's observation (1961, 17) that simple societies are relatively stable (i.e., immobile) due to a high degree of congruence between "what is produced and what is desired" (or in our terms: relevance is rendered controllable), we can assume that the condition of the elderly in such societies is of minimal uncertainty. Indeed, relevant ethnographic material supports this hypothesis as long as "over-aging"[25] does not cleave the old person's world into two discrepant domains.

The construction of uncertainty through the manipulation of control and relevance can be regarded as a regulating principle in which the form, rather than the content, is the fundamental dimension. During the later years of life, when due to personal experience of social disarray, well-established mechanisms of accommodation cease to be effective, newly acquired strategies are put into operation. The apparent shallowness of social relationships observed among old people—the adherence to habits, the recourse to personal worlds of "nostalgia," and the revitalization of old traditions—as well as its opposite, such as the creation of new community life, are all endeavors to reach an existentially valid equilibrium between meanings and related means of control.

This conceptual approach thus adds a new dimension to the corpus of research on the institutionalized aged, which hitherto has been infused with the preconception that the life of elderly inmates is mainly affected by curtailment of power, increased dependency, and limited choice. Usually, adaptation to old-age homes is analyzed in terms of the impact of administrative control,[26] or as a product of multivariable interactions between environmental conditions and

149

individual resources.[27] For the aged, relocation as a potential arena for the reconstruction of reality vis-à-vis the manipulability of relevant life worlds has been generally overlooked. The thesis propounded in this study offers a new perspective into the inner experience of the life world of elderly people, whose self-conception is shaped and constituted through the active management of change and immutability.

The image of isolation and decadence in old-age homes, occasionally alleviated by contacts with the outside world[28] or internal cultural homogeneity,[29] is based on the view that "the spectacle of people living collectively in various stages of senesence, awaiting death, away from family and possessions, seems to be the ultimate tragedy of life" (Puner 1978, 193). Such impressions should be seen as ethnocentric manifestations of the progressive-linear perspectives shared by the non-old. This is not to suggest that institutional care does not entail a considerable measure of anguish and despondency. But it does imply that potentialities for meaningful existence reside even within the reach of those who were doomed to survive under the most severe environmental constraints. This observation makes no claims to novelty: it has been made many times by students of human behavior under stress.[30] Yet it holds a special significance for the understanding of the life of old people, for we tend to project our own values and predelictions onto their world, a world about which much is yet to be debunked and discovered.

The critical contribution of this study is not an attempt to discount or dismiss other perspectives, especially those viewing aging as a dynamic process of exchange and negotiation.[31] It is, however, my conviction that the application of such analytic principles is partial, without questioning the meaning of the theoretical foundations upon which the empirical study of such social relationships is erected. The interplay between relevance and control, as governed by the individual's quest to manage change, renders the behavioral patterns among the aged explicable. It also helps to resolve some of the perplexing paradoxes so commonly interwoven into the analysis of growing old. Thus, senescence can be construed as a static state on the one hand, and yet as a dynamic phenomenon on the other. Linearly, it is indeed immobile, but cyclically, it is fraught with internal movement. It includes elements of both continuity and disengagement, since the content of the life world remains, whereas structural relationships change. It allows for a theoretical bypass

150

from the arid discussions concerning "phases and stages" along the "life course," without becoming tangled in inextricable dilemmas of "crisis," "anomie," "rolelessness," and "role exit." Finally, it helps liberate us from ethnocentric misconceptions, based on nonage-bound models of reality, which distort our understanding of the aged and their world.

Notwithstanding the theoretical properties of the model, it calls for a reexamination of widely implemented policies of advocating and promoting activity among the institutionalized aged. While this issue is beyond the scope of our discussion, its implications concerning the type and extent of social intervention vis-à-vis the creative and generative potential of the elderly should remain open-ended.

IV

Having considered certain aspects of the universal and unique dilemma of the human condition of being old with respect to its diverse manifestations, it is now appropriate to consider some of the general implications of our analysis to the anthropological discourse. Since the present discussion has been grounded on a structural, rather than normative or psychological, assumption, it seems reasonable to suppose that anthropological thought could both help support this type of hypothesis and be fructified by it as well. Such an intellectual endeavor is essential, not only to satisfy the need to account for all human phenomena in terms of anthropological categories, but to fit it into academically approved conceptual models. Its primary value is to demonstrate the relevance of aging, as a social phenomenon, in refining such modes of interpreting the world. In other words, if aging is to qualify as a legitimate anthropological concern, it is important to ascertain its properties within a broader behavioral context. Adjustment, therefore, could be viewed not necessarily as a function of the relationship between self and environment, but as a dialectical process, involving certain basic, apersonal dimensions of culture and society.

Indeed, these two well-worn concepts of culture and society enable us to extend our discussion to the wider realm of anthropological discourse. The two key concepts employed in this study—fields of control and spheres of relevance—seem, by means of con-

151

ceptual extrapolation, to respectively correspond to the notions of "society" and "culture." The former term refers to the forms of social control, group organization, and interactional patterns, while the latter relates to questions of meaning, symbolic construction, and the moral order. Although they are analytic constructs, these two dimensions of social life suggest two distinct existential domains that may loosely be termed the available (real) and the desirable (ideal).

Anthropological literature, and sociological thought as well, is rife with didactical references employing this dichotomy. Yet only rarely are the dialectics of the two dimensions examined simultaneously (for a notable exception, see Cohen 1974). Moreover, the longstanding socioanthropological predicament of how to interrelate the macrolevel of culture and society to the microcosmos of the individual's everyday life has often been glossed over by obscure and fuzzy theoretical frameworks.

If, however, culture and society are regarded as two systems of accountability determining a single range of symbolic commitment and interactional responsibility, then a linkage between the macro and the micro can be established.

The study of the home serves as a test case for such assumptions. The relative sequestration of the residents from the surrounding cultural milieu and their former social arenas loosen the connection with the external social reality, and make the need greater to reestablish the content, extent, and structure of each of these two dimensions, and the relationship between them. Thus the management of any novel or emergent situation may reveal culture and society as viable entities in one's life. The aged in general and those who are relocated to alternative environments such as institutional facilities are apparently sometimes more capable than others to demonstrate the scope and capacities of the possibilities of human beings to shape their own fate.

152

POSTSCRIPT: ACCOUNTS AND ACCOUNTABILITY — REPORTING OLD AGE

Any ethnographic description is a practical execution of an underlying conception of the field in question. Such descriptive practice is explicitly or implicitly guided by a code of documentation subjected to a language within which a certain understanding of the reported reality is shaped and with which communication could be established. It is a complex enterprise of translation which, problematical as it must be, finally transforms the field-data into a cogent framework for reenacting the lives and events observed and absorbed. The process of transforming such lived experience into textual presentation involves decisions as to foci of interest, course of argument, and order of significance. The selection of information, the interconnectedness that pieces it together, and the style that conveys the desired message are all necessary products of mental images and intellectual discourses dominating the ethnographer's understanding of the nature of her or his particular experience. The following attempts to reconstruct the decision-making process leading to the ethnography presented in this book. The importance of these reflective procedures draws on a twofold assumption that predicates a linkage between ethnographic accounts and forms of theoretical accountability. Also, it propounds the special case of reporting old age as a unique issue in ethnographic practice. The available options for framing material will precede the exposition of the final choice that constitutes and justifies the structure, content, and spirit of description and analysis.

At the outset of this study it should be reemphasized that the emergent interpretative paradigm of the discussion is composed of cyclical characteristics, that is to say, that the behavioral patterns detected in the home can be best explained in structurally repetitive terms. The question, therefore, arises as to the faithfulness of the ethnography phrased in conventional linear linguistic codes to an existentially opposite experience. The uncomfortable, yet imperative solution to that problem is the ultimate subject of this section. Since this dilemma is the core of socioanthropological quest for credibility, it deserves a systematic unfolding.

Entering an institution for the aged involves the novice ethnographer in a double-bind situation. Goaded by the anthropological dictate of gaining access of understanding to another universe, he confronts a reality of everyday living underpinned by needs, problems, and sinecure. While the former does not exclude the others and knowledge does not deny empathy, their respective assumed objects do seem to be diametrically opposed to each other. Thus, the exigency to become an advocate of residents complaining about the quality of services in the home could be, and arguably should be, fufilled while doing fieldwork, but must be suppressed or else treated as a piece of ethnographic material in its own right when considering the data. Separating commitment to understanding from advocacy was implemented only at level of writing up where ehtnographic account are made accountable for intellectual discourse. At the level of doing fieldwork, however, separation was neither desirable nor possible and active involvement in the affairs of the institution was inevitable.

Having chosen the sociological direction rather than the social interest, the issue at stake was the manner in which such an approach could be followed. Socioanthropological conviction has it that interpretative models of a given reality must be edified on a contextual foundation. The case of the home offered at least two such contextual frameworks within which data could be organized in a meaningful fashion. The first is the culturally biased perspective of viewing the old as a separate category of people, hence taking age as a measurement for delineating boundaries between "in" and "out," "residents" and "others," "old" and "non-old." Cues for such divisions are embedded in certain anthropological trends (Keith 1980a; Kertzer and Keith 1984; Bernardi 1985) and provide readily accessible markers for social classifications. Taking such an analytic stance would spell a preassumption regarding the inherently different status of the old versus the non-old in the stratification system of society. Furthermore, the grey areas imperatively invoked by that symbolic code of separation might engender subdivisions and blurred cultural zones (Gubrium 1986), whose cultural function defies the notion to which this thesis subscribes—"old people as peo-

154

ple" (Keith 1982). The Israeli scene seems to complicate matters considerably, since distinctions between old and non-old are heavily influenced by intergenerational relations that ignore chronological age and emphasize mythical and political stature (Shapiro 1980).

The setting itself, that of a seemingly total institution, calls for yet another contextual framing. Ethnographic evidence, however, denies any attempt at understanding the experience of living in the home in terms of the peculiar form articulated by Goffman (1961a). Being an impregnable setting to the outside world and, indeed, part and parcel of its structure and dynamics, the home did not conform to the characteristics of a total institution. Nonetheless, a close scrutiny of the ethnographic accounts reveals that the home in question does not display the conventional properties of a total institution. It should be noted, however, that observations in the home unfold a multifaceted view of totality. Some residents are afforded the privilege of treating the institution as a safe and comfortable haven selectively sequestrated and realigned to the extra-institutional universe. Some residents consider the Home as a hotel-like base for a vital connection with the world, while others are forced to regard the home as the hub of their lives and the crux of their future fate. This variability demands the invocation of another perspective.

Both perspectives—the cultural and the social—assume a prevalent relation between the institutionally old and their surrounding counterparts. This kind of discourse induces the linkage between old-age homes and adjustment to old age. Relocation, being the operative term for such a nexus, presumes a dramatic change in attitudes and behavior in the course of transition (Lieberman 1974; Tobin and Lieberman 1976). Old-age homes are thus regarded as arenas for transformation in life histories.

Life histories rendered as life stories constitute a well-established data-base for obtaining an overall picture of a cultural unit or an individual member of it. The abandonment of social context for personal life review underlies the dual anthropological tendency to propound the idea of continuity as overriding other possible variables (Myerhoff and Simic 1978; Kaufman 1986; Frank 1980). It also takes precedence over recent experiments in the "poetics" of ethnographic renditions (Clifford and Marcus 1986). Eschewing all this on the one hand and realizing the importance of adaptability on the other debunks the ethnography of its holdings in a conventional paradigm and calls for a rethinking of the question of the nadir of

155

the research. Particularly disturbing is the need to treat the idea of adjustment without the templates of immediate context. Studies of adjustment to old age, diverse as they are, draw on various environmental measures as indications for modes of adaptability. Thus Gubrium (1973), Rowles (1978), and Lawton (1980) stress the importance of social space for accommodation to later life; Lieberman and Tobin (1983) and Lazarus and Folkman (1984) maintain that daily living conditions are responsible for the loci of stress in old age. Comparative studies in that wake demonstrate how diverse sociocultural milieus shape different sets of human characteristics among the elderly. Kayser-Jones (1981, 1986), Clough (1981), and Francis (1984) all attest to the dominant effect of social networks and cultural resources on the social arenas within which the elderly people operate.

Shunning away from the influence of direct context is a rare property in research on the aged and is usually confined to psychologically oriented approaches. Anthropological perspectives such as those developed by Clark and Anderson (1967) or Kaufman (1986) are among the few analytic scopes that offer cogent models for adaptation without resorting to contextual explanations. It is, indeed, the former work that inspired the argument advanced in this book. Clark and Anderson's contention that adaptation in old age requires a redefinition of goals to social resources and hence a reintergration of the self, could be regarded as the origin of "spheres of relevance" and "fields of control."

However, field experience at the home did not inform the concepts of coherent self and accommodation to a new way of life. Rather, it evinced disjuncture in many spheres of existence ranging from disjointed linguistic expressions through multivocal manifestations of autobiographical narratives to incongruous displays of social interaction. It was evident that communication with the seemingly disarrayed world of residents could not be facilitated by a pretense of empathy or by the application of tried academic models. It became clear that the understanding of the elderly in question must take into account the enigmatic, apparently unintelligible nature of their universe. Short of representing the overtly articulated channel of "functioning" are hidden the undercurrents of life as old rather than that of a resident remain hidden.

The quest for the special language of old age is guided by the puzzlement of the unique cultural status of the aged as being between and betwixt life and death (see, for example, Hazan 1980a; Elias 1985). Aries (1983) advocated that preindustrial societies did not hold death at bay and that awareness of termination of somatic existence accompanied almost any act of everyday life. In our society, where cessation of corporeal existence is removed, sequestrated, and distanced from the life course, the elderly incarnate the buffer zone between the living and the dead.

The territorial enclave of a culturally ill-defined space baffles the enthnographer whose objective is to translate apparent uncertainty to the seemingly certain and solid jargon of anthropoloigcal discourse. It was a task beyond words and action. The only anthropological model that availed itself to such description was that of rites of passage (Van-Gennep [1908] 1960; Turner 1969) where words and action are halted and broken.

Uncovering the language of confronting unilateral change invoked the question of the validity of ethnographic representation in its relation to observable reality (Fabian 1983). It was thus decided that rather than adhering to fold-models and to emic locutions, relative justice to the enigmatic inaccessible nature of the subject matter could be done through enlising the most remote, yet accurate, rendition of the people under study. It became the goal of the study to explore the methods of the old "explorers," and, rather than answering Butler's (1975) perennial question "Why survive?", it reverts to the inexorable tenet that, in the words of T. S. Eliot, "here and now cease to matter."

NOTES

NOTES TO INTRODUCTION

1. Maddox's (1979) succinct review of social gerontological literature exemplifies the abundance and pervasiveness of the treatment of the concept of adjustment or adaptation in the research on aging. A critical perspective to themes of "socialization" and "resocialization" is offered by Rosow (1974).

2. For an elucidation of this approach see, for example, Fontana (1976) and Marshall (1979).

3. It would be presumptuous to attempt to summarize the various perspectives pertaining to this conceptualization. It is sufficient to say that it draws on symbolic interaction, phenomenology, and ethnomethodology, or what Dawe (1974) terms "sociology of control," which postulates the processional struggle in human endeavor to control the meanings attributed by an individual to his life. Philosophically, it is a branch of what Johnson and Douglas (1977) called "existential sociology." I have deliberately avoided direct reference to the conceptual framework of symbolic interaction, particularly Goffman's version of it, since the case of the elderly poses certain fundamental problems as to the validity of the analysis of "self" versus "significant others" (see: Conclusion).

4. A term coined by Burgess (1950), expounded and developed as "role exit" by Blau (1974).

5. A concept embedded in a wide scope of gerontological literature, explicated by Fontana (1976).

6. See Rosow (1974).

7. For an elaboration of this argument, see Hazan (1980a).

8. See Myerhoff and Simic (1978) and Marshall (1979).

9. See, for example, Henry's description of two American nursing homes (1961), or Townsend's survey of institutions for the care of the aged in England and Wales (1964).

10. Perhaps the most noteworthy study of the phenomenon is Mendelson's (1975).

11. See Hess and Markson (1980, 153–55).

12. For an analysis of power and control in old-age homes, see Bennett and Nahemow (1965).

13. See Sommer (1969).

14. For example: Shanas et al.'s (1962) observation that old people regard institutionalization as a stage preceding death.

15. A sociological drive advocated in various areas of the discipline, particularly the Weberian school with its emphasis on existential problems. A more structural approach to the issue is propounded by Goffman (1974), a perspective that is also our theoretical premise.

16. For reviews of the literature, see Fry (1980), Keith (1980a), and Spencer (1990).

NOTES TO CHAPTER 1

1. This is supported by a statement made at a convention of physiotherapists, namely that "there is a shocking shortage of places in old-age homes"—*Ma'ariv*, 6 July 1972.

2. Mishan—a welfare division of the Histadrut, the biggest trade union federation in Israel; Malben—an organization operating geriatric institutions administered by the Jewish Agency and hence designated to cater mainly for the needs of elderly new immigrants.

3. Support for this statement can be found in Townsend's survey in which he found that only twenty-six percent of the residents in old-age homes who had roommates were interested in perpetuating the arrangement. The reason for this, in his opinion, is the desire to protect individuality within the institutional framework (Townsend 1964, 181). As will be seen, this problem is central in the institution under study.

4. Today, following the establishment of the new facility, this assertion is probably inaccurate, but even at the time of the report Mishan had connections with institutions for the chronically sick and several cases were directed to them.

5. Support for this view was expressed by the director-general of the Ministry of Welfare when interviewed in the Israeli Radio (27 February 1973).

6. When the study began the cost was as follows: for a single room: entrance fee IL.7,000, monthly charge IL.320; for a double room: entrance fee IL.3,000, monthly charge IL.300. (IL. i.e., Israeli lira. Israeli currency at the time of research was equivalent approximately to U.S. $2.00.)

7. Other questions related to these can be asked, such as: How do these conditions affect relations between the residents and the staff or, even more importantly, how does this problem express itself in group organization in the institution? These matters will receive detailed consideration in the presentation of subsequent material.

8. As an example, the manager cited the struggle between several homes over the privilege of admitting a distinguished author, despite the fact that he was immobile toward the end of his life.

9. Details of this matter will appear below.

10. Data that might have clarified the profile of the population of the home were unobtainable because they were either not entered at all on the resident's filing card, or were partial or faulty. The problem is not specific to this home, as Weihl notes, ". . . much needed information was unobtainable because it was not included in the files" (Weihl et al. 1970, 213).

11. All the comparative data are taken from Weihl et al. (1970).

12. The problem of the institutionalization of Histadrut veterans prompted Mishan to decide to establish a new institution catering only to this category.

13. This category has been particularly mentioned because people from these countries play a leading role in the social life of the home.

14. The extent to which a change in the internal structure of an old-age home can affect the social behavior of its residents can be seen in Sommer's article, "Designed for Refuge and Behavior Change" (1969, 77–97).

15. See below for details of events connected with this phenomenon and others of a similar nature.

16. Development of this theme with additional data will be presented in the description of congregants in the synagogue.

17. The fact that a number of residents owned automobiles attests to the considerable differences among the population in "mobility potential" outside the institution.

18. For an example of this kind of criticism, see the description of the discussion group.

19. This will be discussed in detail later.

NOTES TO CHAPTER 2

1. For example, Fontana (1976), Myerhoff and Simic (1978), Myerhoff (1979), and Hazan (1980a).

2. A more accurate interpretation of the significance of the various uses of nomenclature, by whom and when, will be given in the chapters on group activity.

3. Goffman (1961a) describes a similarly defined situation arising between staff and inmates with the former viewing the latter as nonhuman. This sort of perspective, which also prevails among some residents toward others, renders clarification of the relations between residents an issue of paramount importance in the understanding of the total institution.

4. This phenomenon is similar both in structure and outcome to Steiner's description (1967) of the process of taboo-formation in tribal societies.

5. Goffman (1959) coined the term, and descriptions embodying its use in regard to the dying or to those expelled from society can be found in Sudnow (1970), Kalish (1968), and Miller and Gwynne (1972).

6. Support for this view can be found also in the studies conducted on the relations between young people toward their elders, and they reveal that these tendencies are predominantly negative (see, for example, Tuckman et al.(1961), Kagan and Sheldon (1962), and Kastenbaum and Durkee (1964a, 1964b).

7. A similar topic is dealt with in the description of family visits in a retired residents' community studied by Ross (1977).

8. A similar phenomenon is described by Johnson (1971) when "successful" children raise their parents' prestige through the exchange of photographs.

9. The Histadrut's daily newspaper.

10. Meaning: "The Fathers' Word."

11. The composition of the editorial board and its proximity to the manager makes the search for material selective, and therefore it should not be considered an accurate reflection of reality within the institution.

12. This kind of reflective behavior by the elderly can be explained mainly with the help of an understanding of the social context in which they

162

are being examined, and with reference to this particular old-age home the matter is clear-cut (for the complete picture see the chapter on the "discussion group"). This contradicts the approach that equates the recollections of old people with purely psychological factors such as the sense of approaching death, etc. See, for example, Butler (1964, 274).

13. The organized Jewish population in Palestine before 1948.

14. A Jewish holiday celebrated on the fourteenth of Adar, the sixth month of the Hebrew calendar. Fancy dress and frivolity are customary on that day.

15. Certain residents are also at the "receiving end" of sarcastic remarks and teasing comments. For instance, a greeting to one female resident went as follows: "I want her to listen to music, even if it emanates from our choir."

16. See the section on the significance of newspaper reading in the home.

17. See the previous reference in chapter 1.

18. For a more complete picture, see the chapter on the material living conditions within the home and also the chapter describing the discussion group.

19. A treatment of this question can be found on Coser's article, "A Home Away from Home" (1956).

NOTES TO CHAPTER 3

1. Concerning the background to this approach and the manager's need to justify it, see chapter 1.

2. This study deals only with groups operating in a predetermined framework and with the management's blessing. Primary groups of residents, informal groups, etc., will not be discussed.

3. All the names mentioned hereafter are fictitious.

4. See the affair of the steward, Mr. Mizrahi, in the chapter on the synagogue.

5. The significance of reference groups for the elderly as models for norms of role definition and for evaluation was emphasized, for example, by Rosow (1967, 135–40), not in the context of institutional life, but from a community standpoint.

6. Another way of looking at relations between residents and staff is proposed by Fox (1959, 241), who presents "family" relations in the setting of a hospital ward. It seems that this approach, which arises from the special nature of the metabolic ward in which the study was carried out, is not relevant to old-age homes.

7. See, for instance, the chapter on the occupational group: Mrs. Shimoni and Mr. Nahmani.

8. This is contrary to consistent findings in gerontological literature: "One of the most consistent findings of surveys of old people is their refusal to acknowledge that they are old" (Rosow 1974, 117).

NOTES TO CHAPTER 4

1. This question and those following are raised by Edgerton (1963, 385) where they refer to open-ended issues that the author proposes for further study in the wake of his research of the elite in an institution for the mentally retarded.

2. The source of the quotation is not disclosed in order to prevent identification of the people involved.

3. The Jewish Brigade—a volunteer force that fought in the Second World War.

4. Haganah—the "official" underground volunteer defense organization of the Jewish Agency—the government-in-the-making before the establishment of the State of Israel.

5. Nachshonim.

6. Nefilim.

7. "The Labor stream": Before the establishment of the State of Israel, the General Federation of Labor (Histadrut) had its own school system that emphasized socialist-Zionist values. After the establishment of Israel, the "networks" were abolished and all elementary schools came under the jurisdiction of the State.

8. As we saw in the first chapter, many people think there is no justification for an institution for the able-bodied elderly.

9. The manner in which the meeting was run strengthens the contention that the pattern of behavior witnessed at group meetings was adopted from that of similar gatherings in which they took part prior to entering the

164

home (it is even possible that this simulation is exaggerated, but I have no way of checking it).

10. This kind of language is very unusual in the home, where great care is taken both by staff and residents to use the terms "old-age home" or "institution." It is possible that by using this objectionable designation the manager intended to emphasize the value and nature of his home and in so doing to dampen the criticism that was likely to be directed at him.

11. It seems that this process of rationalization was part of a process of coping with the cognitive dissonance to which many members of the group were subject.

12. Another possible explanation, which seems to me tenuous, is to attribute the loyalty to the homogeneous institution to the fear of its transformation into a heterogeneous variant, where they would have to cope with a professional staff that would be more impervious to pressure and less amenable to interference in its judgmental processes.

13. This bears out the assumption that was made in the analysis of the previous episode whereby support of the manager is not necessarily a result of a desire to enhance his power.

14. The staff-resident polarization and the process of abasement described in the episode are designed by residents as measures against the manager and as such it describes a situation the opposite of that described by Goffman (1961a) in the institution he studied, where he found such situations to be the result of the staff's perception of the residents.

15. It is conceivable that this accounts for the nonparticipation of Mr. Reuveni, the blind man, in the group meetings, despite the fact that a number of group members are his personal friends.

16. On the importance of a psychological criterion for facilitating interpersonal discrimination and the development of groups based on it, see Cleveland and Fisher (1968, 206).

NOTES TO CHAPTER 5

1. See details of this in the first chapter.

2. For a comparison, see the discussion on the home's newspaper at the end of chapter 2.

3. See chapter 4.

4. This matter is explained in terms of the existing rivalry between Mishan and Malben, in which the ability to incorporate the elderly into an

occupational framework is one of the main points of contention. For details see chapter 1.

NOTES TO CHAPTER 6

1. In conversation with synagogue-goers on the significance of their attendance, many denied any connection with private suffering, death, and so on. During the High Holidays, on the other hand, considerable feeling accompanied by spasmodic weeping could be discerned when the following prayer passages were read: "Do not abandon me during my old age," and "Grant us a complete recovery." At any rate, I do not possess material that would allow a well-grounded, systematic examination of the subject.

2. It is possible that the motives of the members of the discussion group for continuing to maintain political activity in the home were no weaker than those of the religious grouping; but the channels and patterns of such activity, by their very nature, were more stringent and inflexible.

3. According to Geertz's (1965) definition, it is possible to see in this activity religion-inspired action since it comprises the two basic elements essential to this definition: a symbol that reacts to an existential problem (lingering on in the home and self, as well as social evaluation in the institutional framework). From an analytic standpoint, this reference to the symbol is "innovative" (Deshen 1970, 266). In no case should this activity be seen as "survival" or "ritualism," because despite the earlier impoverishment in content associated with this activity, it is defined within another sphere of meaning that explains its perpetuation.

4. This sentence possibly makes explicit the reason for the estranged attitude of the residents towards the man. The words "and this is what one expects to find in it" conveys a similar kind of view to that attributed by Goffman (1961a), as precisely characterizing that of members of the staff, whose main element is the labelling of inmates as objects and nonhuman entities.

NOTES TO CHAPTER 7

1. See note 9 to the Introduction.

2. For a review of the relevant ethnographic studies, see Keith (1980b).

3. As opposed to Thomae (1976), who regards "achievements" and "desires" as two separable entities.

166

4. For a review of the life-stages perspective, see Kimmel (1974). A more structural, sociological approach is proposed by Riley and Foner (1968).

5. See, for example, Rosow's (1976) succinct review of role-related approaches to aging.

6. A theme underpinning a great deal of socioanthropological material. A noteworthy example is Roth's (1963) analysis of constructing uncertainty in terms of scheduling.

7. Unless anomie and disorganization are regarded as desirable states, this postulate cannot be challenged or invalidated.

8. See, for example, Ross (1975), Fry (1979), and Keith (1980b).

9. See Myerhoff (1979) and Myerhoff and Simic (1978).

10. Simmel's "formal sociology" as exemplified in his analysis of various phenomena can be taken as a general framework for our approach.

11. The term "ecology of the mind" is most apt to locate Bateson's mode of analysis within ours. It also conveys cogently the idea of the individual as an arena for the operation of structural influences.

12. See Goffman's (1974) and Sharon's criticism (1981) of the lack of temporality in the concept. Such criticism, however, reaffirms our view of the relevance of this analytic device to the understanding of atemporality.

13. See Turner (1969).

14. The phenomenon of cognitively arresting the flow of events is described in a few studies. See, for example, Seeley et al. (1956), Doob (1971, 370–412), Musgrove (1976), and Hazan (1980a).

15. A phenomenological term much used recently in the ethnomethodological literature, describing the annulment of the gap between subject and object.

16. For instance, a reanalysis of Fontana's (1976) three studies could lend itself to such interpretation.

17. Particularly Handelman's (1977) study of play among the aged.

18. See, for example, Hanna (1977).

19. See Blumenstiel (1973).

20. Particularly Turner's concept of the state of communitas as being "in and out of time" or an "atemporal" condition (Turner 1974, 35–37).

167

21. A theme developed by Mead (1932).

22. For an elaboration of this theme, see Hazan (1980b).

23. For a critical perspective on the theory, see Hochschild (1975).

24. See note 4.

25. For an account of the consequences of such categorization, see Glascock and Feiman (1980).

26. See note 12 to the Introduction.

27. Such an approach has been developed by Moos (1981).

28. Glaser and Strauss (1968), Kosberg (1973), and Gottesman and Bourestom (1974) observed that those residents who manage to maintain contact with the outside world also receive relatively more care and attention than others who are isolated.

29. Kahana and Harel (1972) and Hendel-Sebestein (1979) found that shared cultural heritage leads to highly intensive relationships between residents and promotes a feeling of solidarity among them.

30. A most notable example is to be found in Frankel's experience and theory (1963).

31. An exchange theory is applied to aging by Dowd (1975) and Bengston and Dowd (1980).

REFERENCES

Aries, P.
1983   *The Hour of Our Death*. London: Penguin.

Arkin, N.
1973   Aging is not a Predestination. *Maàriv*, April 4th, p. 33. In Hebrew.

Bachi, R.
1971   The Aged Population in Israel. In *In Time of Old Age*, edited by S. Bergman, 7–16. Tel-Aviv, Israel: Gerontological Association. In Hebrew.

Belknap, I.
1956   *The Human Problems of a State Mental Hospital*. New York: McGraw-Hill.

Bengston V., and J. Dowd.
1980   Sociological Functionalism, Exchange Theory and Life Cycle Analysis: A Call for More Explicit Theoretical Bridges. *International Journal of Aging and Human Development* 12:55–73.

Bennett, R.
1963   The Meaning of Institutional Life. *The Gerontologist* 3:117–25.

Bennett R., and L. Nehamow.
1965   Institutional Totality and Criteria of Social Adjustment in Residences for the Aged. *Journal of Social Issues* 21 (no. 4): 44–79.

Bernardi, B.
1985   *Age Class Systems: Social Institutions and Politics Based on Age*. Cambridge: Cambridge University Press.

Blau, Z. S.
1974   *Old Age in a Changing Society*. New York: New Viewpoints.

Blumenstiel, A.
1973   The Sociology of Good Times. In *Phenomenological Sociology*, edited by G. Psathas, 187–218. New York: John Wiley.

Brookdale Institute of Gerontology & Adult Human Development—
Joint Israel
1982   *Aging in Israel*. A chartbook prepared by Brookdale staff, Jerusalem.

Burgess, E.
1950   Personal and Social Adjustment in Old Age. In *The Aged and Society*, edited by M. Derber, 138–56. Illinois: Industrial Relations Research, Association.

Butler, R.
1964   The Life-Review—An Interpretation of Reminiscence in the Aged. In *New Thoughts on Old Age*, edited by R. Kastenbaum, 265–80. New York: Springer.

Butler, R.
1975   *Why Survive?—Being Old in America*. New York: Harper & Row.

Clark, M., and B. G. Anderson.
1967   *Culture and Aging: An Anthropological Study of Older Americans*. Springfield, Illinois: Charles Thomas.

Cleveland, S., and S. Fisher.
1968   *Body Image and Personality*. New York: Dover.

Clifford, J., and G. Marcus, eds.
1986   *Writing Culture: The Poetics and Politics of Ethnography*. Berkeley: University of California Press.

Clough, R.
1981   *Old Age Homes*. London: George Allen and Unwin.

Cohen, A.
1974   *Two Dimensional Man*. London: Routledge and Kegan Paul.

Coser, R.
1964   A Home Away from Home. *Social Problems* 4:3–17.

Cowgill, D. O., and L. D. Holmes, (eds.)
1972   *Aging and Modernization*. New York: Appleton Century.

Cumming, E., and W. E. Henry.
1961   *Growing Old: The Process of Disengagement*. New York: Basic Books.

Dawe, D.
1974   The Two Sociologies. *British Journal of Sociology* 21:207–18.

Deshen, S.
1970   On Religious Change: The Situational Analysis of Symbolic Action. *Comparative Studies in Society and History* 12 (no. 3): 260–74.

Doob, L.
1971   *Patterning of Time*. New Haven: Yale University Press.

Douglas, M.
1968   The Social Control of Cognition: Some Factors in Joke Perception. *Man* 3:361–77.
1970   *Natural Symbols: Explanations in Cosmology*. London: Penguin.

Dowd, J.
1975   Aging as Exchange: A Preface to Theory. *Journal of Gerontology* 30:584–95.

Dunham, H. W., and S. K. Weinberg.
1960   *The Culture of the State Mental Hospital*, Detroit Mental Hospital, Detroit, Wayne State University Press.

Edgerton, R. B.
1963   A Patient Elite: Ethnography in a Hospital for the Mentally Retarded. *American Journal of Mental Deficiency* 68 (no. 4):372–85.

Elias, N.
1985   *The Loneliness of the Dying*. Oxford: Basil Blackwell.

Etzioni, E.
1964   *Modern Organizations*. Englewood Cliffs, New-Jersey: Prentice-Hall.

Fabian, J.
1983   *Time and the Other: How Anthropology Makes Its Object*. New York: Columbia University Press.

Fontana, A.
1976   *The Last Frontier*. Beverly Hills: Sage.

Fox, R. C.
1959   *Experiment Perilous: Physicians and Patients Facing the Unknown*. Glencoe, Illinois: The Free Press.

Francis, D.
1984   *Will You Still Need Me, Will You Still Feed Me When I am 84?* Bloomington: Indiana University Press.

171

Frank, G.
1980   Life Histories in Gerontology, the Subjective Side of Aging. In *New Methods for Old Age Research, Anthropological Alternatives*, edited by C. L. Fry and J. Keith, 155–76. Chicago, Loyola University.

Frankel, V.
1963   *Man's Search for Meaning*. New York: Pocket Books.

Fry, C.
1979   Structural Conditions Affecting Community Formation Among the Aged. *Anthropological Quarterly* 52:7–18.
1980   Toward an Anthropology of Aging. In *Aging in Culture and Society*, edited by C. Fry, 1–20. New York: J. F. Bergin.

Geertz, C.
1965   Religion as a Cultural System. In *Reader in Comparative Religion*, edited by W. Lessa and E. Vogt, 204–16. New York: Harper and Row.

Giallombardo, R.
1966   Social Roles in a Prison for Women. *Social Problems* 13:268–88.

Glascock, A., and S. Feiman.
1980   Social Asset or Social Burden: Treatment of the Aged in Nonindustrial Society. In *Dimensions: Aging, Culture and Health*, edited by C. Fry, 13–32. New York, Praeger.

Glaser, B., and A. Strauss.
1968   *Time for Dying*. Chicago: Aldine.

Gluckman, M.
1960   *Custom and Conflict in Africa*. Oxford: Blackwell.

Goffman, E.
1959   *The Presentation of Self in Everyday Life*. Garden City, New York: Doubleday.
1961a   On the Characteristics of Total Institutions. In *Asylums: Essays on the Social Situation of Mental Patients and Other Inmates*, 1–124. New York: Anchor Books.
1961b   The Underlife of a Public Institution. In *Asylums: Essays on the Social Situation of Mental Patients and Other Inmates*, 171–320. New York: Anchor Books.
1961c   The Moral Career of a Mental Patient. In *Asylums: Essays on the Social Situation of Mental Patients and Other Inmates*, 125–170. New York: Anchor Books.
1968   *Stigma*. London: Penguin.
1974   *Frame Analysis*. New York: Harper and Row.

Gottesman L., and N. Bourestom.
1974   Why Nursing Homes Do What They Do? *The Gerontologist* 14:501–
        06.

Gubrium, J.
1973   *The Myth of the Golden Years: A Socio-Environmental Theory of
        Aging.* Springfield, Illinois: Charles C. Thomas.
1975   *Living and Dying at Murray Manor.* New York: St. Martin's Press.
1986   *Oldtimers and Alzheimers: The Descriptive Organization of Se-
        nility.* Greenwich, Conn. JAI Press.

Gubrium J., and D. Buckholdt.
1977   *Towards Maturity.* San Francisco: Jossey-Bass.

Guttman, D.
1964   An Exploration of Ego Configuration in Middle and Late Life. In
        Personality in Middle and Late Life, edited by B. Neugarten. New-
        York: Atherton.

Guttman, D.
1969   The Country of Old Man: Cross Cultural Studies in the Psychology
        of Late Life. In *Occasional Papers in Gerontology*, edited by W.
        Donahue, 1–37. Ann Arbor, Michigan: Ann Arbor Institute of
        Gerontology.

Handelman, D.
1977   *Work and Play Among the Aged.* Amsterdam: Van-Gorcum.

Hanna J.
1977   To Dance is Human. In *The Anthropology of the Body*, edited by J.
        Blacking, 211–32. London: Academic Press.

Harpaz, H.
1978   *Characteristics, Attitudes and Needs of the Old People in Tel-Aviv-
        Yafo.* Tel-Aviv: Tel-Aviv Center for Economic and Social Research,
        Tel-Aviv-Yafo Municipality and Israel Gerontological Society.

Hazan, H.
1980a   *The Limbo People: A Study of the Constitution of the Time Universe
        among the Aged.* London: Routledge and Kegan Paul.
1980b   Continuity and Change in a Teacup: On the Symbolic Nature of Tea-
        Related Behaviour Among the Aged. *The Sociological Review*
        28:497–518.

Hendel-Sebestein, G.
1979   Role Diversity: Toward a Development of Community in a Total
        Institutional Setting. *Anthropological Quarterly* 52:19–28.

173

Henry, J.
1961   *Culture Against Man*. London: Penguin.

Hess, B., and W. Markson.
1980   *Aging and Old Age*. New York: Macmillan.

Hochschild, A.
1975   Disengagement Theory: A Critique and Proposal. *American Sociological Review* 40:553–69.

Israel Government Year Book.
1972   Jerusalem: The Ministry of Education. In Hebrew.

Israel Statistical Annual.
1970   Jerusalem: Central Bureau of Statistics. In Hebrew.

Johnson, S.
1971   *Idle Haven*. Berkeley: University of California Press.

Johnson, J., and J. Douglas.
1977   *Existential Sociology*. Cambridge: Cambridge University Press.

Kahana E., and Z. Harel.
1972   Social and Behavioral Principles in Residential Care Settings for the Aged: The Residents' Perspective. Presented at the Annual Meeting of American Orthopsychiatric Association, Detroit.

Kagan, N., and F. Sheldon.
1962.   "Beliefs about Old People—A Comparative Study of Older and Younger Samples" in: *The Journal of Genetic Psychology* 100:93–111.

Kalish, R.
1968   Life and Death—Dividing the Indivisible. *Social Science and Medicine* 2:249–59.

Kastenbaum R., and N. Durkee.
1964a   Elderly People View Old Age. In *New Thoughts on Old Age*, edited by R. Kastenbaum, 251–62. New York: Springer.
1964b.   Young People View Old Age. In *New Thoughts on Old Age*, edited by R. Kastenbaum, 237–49. New York, Springer.

Kaufman, S.
1986   *The Ageless Self: Sources of Meaning in Later Life*. Madison: University of Wisconsin Press.

Kayser-Jones, J.
1981   *Old, Alone and Neglected: Care of The Aged in Scotland and the United States*. Berkeley: University of California Press.

174

1986   Open-Ward Accommodation in Long-Term Care Facility: The Elderly Point of View. *The Gerontologist* 26:63–69.

Keith, J.
1980a   The Best is Yet To Be: Toward an Anthropology of Age. *Annual Review of Anthropology* 9:339–64.
1980b   Old Age and Community Creation. In *Aging in Culture and Society*, edited by C. Fry, 170–97. New York: J. F. Bergin.
1982   *Old People as People: Social and Cultural Influences on Aging and Old Age*. Boston and Toronto: Little, Brown.

Kenan, N.
1973   Breaking Through the Circle of Loneliness. *Dvar Hashavua*, January 26, pp. 18–19. In Hebrew.

Kertzer, D., and J. Keith.
1984   *Age and Anthropological Theory*. Ithaca: Cornell University Press.

Kimmel, D.
1974   *Adulthood and Aging*. New York: John Wiley.

Kleenier, R.
1961   *Aging and Leisure*. New York: Oxford University Press.

Kosberg, J.
1973   Differences in Proprietary Institutions Caring for Affluent and Non-affluent Elderly. *The Gerontologist* 13 (part 1):299–304.

Lawton, M. P.
1980   *Environment and Aging*. Monterey, CA: Brooks/Cole Brooks-Cole Publishing Co.

Lazarus, R. S., and S. Folkman.
1984   *Stress Appraisal and Coping*. New York: Springer.

Librach, G.
1974   Services for the Elderly in Israel. In *Geriatrics Gerontology*, edited by A. Brand-Aurban, 48–56. Jerusalem: The Jerusalem Academy of Medicine. In Hebrew.

Lieberman, M. A.
1974   Relocation Research and Social Policy. *The Gerontologist* 14:194–501.

Lieberman, M. A., and S. S. Tobin.
1983   *The Experience of Old Age: Stress, Coping and Survival*. New York: Basic Books.

Maddox, G.
1979   Sociology of Later Life. *Annual Review of Sociology* 5:113–35.

Marshall, V.
1979   No Exit: A Symbolic Interactionalist Perspective of Aging. *International Journal of Aging and Human Development* 9:345–58.

Mead, G.
1932   *The Philosophy of the Present.* Chicago: Open Court Publishing.

Mendelson, M.
1975   *Tender, Loving Greed.* New York: Vintage Books.

Miller, E. J., and G. V. Gwynne.
1972   *A Life Apart: A Pilot Study of Residential Institutions for the Physically Handicapped and the Young Chronic Sick.* London: Tavistock.

Moberg, D., and M. Taves
1965   Church Participation and Adjustment in Old Age. In *Older People and Their Social World,* edited by R. Rose and W. Peterson, 113–24. Philadelphia: F. A. Davis.

Moore, S.
1975   Epilogue: Uncertainty in Situations, Indeterminacies in Culture. In *Symbol and Politics in Community Ideology,* edited by S. Moore and B. G. Myerhoff, 210–39. Ithaca: Cornell University Press.

Moos, R. H.
1981   Environmental Choice and Control in Community Care Settings for Older People. *Journal of Applied Social Psychology* 11(1):23–43.

Moves, P.
1960   Aging, Religion and the Church. In *Handbook of Social Gerontology,* edited by C. Tibbitz, 708–09. Chicago: The University of Chicago Press.

Musgrove, F.
1976   A Home for the Disabled: Marginality and Reality. *British Journal of Sociology* 27 (no. 4):444–60.

Myerhoff, B. G., and A. Simic.
1978   *Life's Career—Aging: Cultural Variations on Growing Old.* Beverly Hills, Sage.

Myerhoff, B.
1979   *Number our Days.* New York: Dutton.

Nathan, T.
1970   "Housing of the Elderly" in H. Weihl (Principal Investigator), *Investigation of the Family Life, Living Conditions and Needs of the Non-Institutionalized Urban Jewish Aged 65+ in Israel, Final Report Part 1*, 114–40. State of Israel: Ministry of Social Welfare.

Nitzan, A.
1970   Demographic Aspects of Aging. In *Geriatrics Gerontology*, edited by A. Brand-Aurban, 26–31. Jerusalem: Israeli Academy of Medicine.

Puner, M.
1978   *To the Good Long Life*. London: Macmillan.

Riley, M., and A. Foner.
1968   *Aging and Society*. Vol. 1. New York: Russell Sage.

Rosengren, W. E., and M. Lefton.
1969   *Hospitals and Patients*. New York: Atherton.

Rosow, I.
1967   *Social Integration of the Aged*. New York: The Free Press.

1974   *Socialization to Old Age*. Berkeley: University of California Press.
1976   Status and Role Change Through the Life Span. In *Handbook of Aging and the Social Sciences*, edited by R. Binstock and E. Shanas, 457–82. New York: Van Nostrand Reinhold.

Ross, J.
1975   Social Borders: Definitions of Diversity. *Current Anthropology*, 16:53–72.
1977   *Old People—New Lives*. Chicago: University of Chicago Press.

Roth, J. A.
1963   *Timetables Structuring the Passage of Time in Hospital Treatment and Other Careers*. Indianapolis: Bobbs-Merrill.

Rowles, G. D.
1978   *Prisoners of Space?* Boulder: Westview Press.

Schneider, D. M.
1965   Some Muddles in the Models; or How the System Really Works. In *The Relevance of Models for Social Anthropology*, edited by M. Banton, 25–86. London, Tavistock.

Seeley, J., et al.
1956   *Crestwood Heights*. New York: Basic Books.

Shanas, E., et al.
1962   *The Health of Older People: A Social Survey.* Cambridge: Harvard University Press.

Shapiro, Y.
1980   Generational Units and Intergenerational Relations in Israeli Politics. In *Israel—A Developing Society*, edited by A. Arian, 161–79. Assen, Van Gorcum.

Sharon, A.
1981   Frame Analysis: When Time Stands Still. *Social Research* 48:500–20.

Simmons, L. W.
1945   *The Role of the Aged in Primitive Society.* New Haven: Yale University Press.

Sommer, R.
1969   *Personal Space: The Behavioral Basis of Design.* Englewood Cliffs, New Jersey: Prentice Hall.

Spencer, P.
1990   The Riddled Course: Theories of Age and its Transformations. In *Anthropology and the Riddle of the Sphinx: Paradoxes of Change in the Life Course.* London: Routledge.

Statistical Abstract of Israel.
1972, 1975, 1978.   Central bureau of statistics, Israel, Jerusalem.

Steiner, F.
1967   *Taboo.* London: Penguin.

Stern, Y.
1972   A 65 Years Old Person Does Not Need to go to an Old Age Home. *Maàriv*, June 8, p. 16. In Hebrew.

Strauss, A., et al.
1963   "The Hospital and its Negotiated Order" in E. Freidson (ed.), *The Hospital in Modern Society*, London, The Free Press.

Sudnow, D.
1970   The Hospital and its Negotiated Order. In *The Hospital in Modern Society*, edited by E. Freidson. London: The Free Press.

Sykes, G. M.
1966   *The Society of Captives—A Study of a Maximum Security Prison.* New York: Atheneum.

Tal, N.
1973   The Scandal of Old Age Homes. *Haàretz*, May 3, p. 12. In Hebrew.

Thomae H.
1976   Bonn Longitudinal Study of Ageing. *Contributions to Human Development*. Vol. 3, Basel, Karger.

Tobin, S. S., and M. A. Lieberman.
1976   *Last Home for the Aged*. San Franciso: Jossey-Bass.

Townsend, P.
1961   *The Family Life of Old People*. London: Penguin.
1964   *The Last Refuge—A Survey of Residential Institutions and Homes for the Aged in England and Wales*. London: Routledge and Kegan Paul.

Tuckman J., et al.
1961   The Self-Image in Aging. *The Journal of Genetic Psychology* 99:317–21.

Turner, V. W.
1969   *The Ritual Process—Structure and Anti-Structure*. London, Routledge and Kegan Paul.
1974   *Dramas, Fields and Metaphors: Symbolic Action in Human Society*. Ithaca: Cornell University Press.

Van Gennep, A.
1960   (1908) *The Rites of Passage*. Translated by M. B. Visedom and G. L. Caffee. Chicago: University of Chicago Press, Phoenix Books.

Wallace, S. E.
1971   On the Totality of Total Institutions. In *Total Institutions*, edited by S. Wallace, 1–8. New Brunswick, New Jersey: Transaction Books.

Weihl, H., et al.
1970   Housing of the Elderly. In *Investigation of the Family Life, Living Conditions and Needs of the Non-Institutionalized Urban Jewish Aged 65+ in Israel, Final Report Part 1*, H. Weihl, Principal Investigator, 212–21. State of Israel: Ministry of Social Welfare.

Weiner, Z.
1968   *Mishan For Any Time—The Story of Mishan*. Tel-Aviv: Mishan Centre. In Hebrew.

Zilberstein, Y.
1967   *Report of the Sub-Committee on the Aged*. Jerusalem: Intra-Ministerial Committee for the Coordination of Social Services. In Hebrew.

INDEX

21.70